a. r.   **DATE DUE**   2/94

~~DE 18 '92~~		
~~AP 2 8 03~~		
AP 2 9 ~~10~~		

DEMCO 38-296

FUJIWARA TEIKA'S
Superior Poems of Our Time

画所領正五位下藤原光方

Fujiwara Teika. A copy by Tosa Mitsuyoshi (1700–1772) of an original portrait attributed to Fujiwara Nobuzane (1177–1265), one of Teika's pupils and a famous painter.

FUJIWARA TEIKA'S
Superior Poems of Our Time

A Thirteenth-Century Poetic Treatise and Sequence

Translated, with an Introduction and Notes,

by Robert H. Brower and Earl Miner

1967
Stanford University Press
Stanford, California

© 1967 by the Board of Trustees of the
Leland Stanford Junior University
Printed by Stanford University Press
Stanford, California, U.S.A.
L.C. 67-17300

To

Sir George Sansom

1883–1965

In Affectionate Memory

PREFACE

We have long felt a special interest in the literary history and poetic achievement of the late twelfth and early thirteenth centuries—the period known in Japan as the Age of the *Shin-kokinshū*. This great neoclassical period was an age of lively criticism and poetic controversy, and it produced the richest and most subtle poetry in Japanese, as well as some of the best. The many fine poets of the period stand out with unusual sharpness against the homogeneous background of the conventional Court style; each of them has a palpably distinct poetic manner.

Among the poets and critics of the Age of the *Shinkokinshū*, Fujiwara Teika is preeminent. His *Superior Poems of Our Time* is not only a miniature anthology of eighty-three poems that he particularly esteemed; it is a major document of Japanese poetics, with a historical significance far beyond its modest physical dimensions. The interest of the work to scholars and specialists unquestionably resides largely in its historical importance. At the same time, *Superior Poems of Our Time* has an intrinsic value as one of the finest examples of a sequence of individual poems skillfully integrated into an esthetic whole. Not every reader may share our concern with Teika and the history of his period, or find this or that individual poem in the anthology particularly to his taste, but we hope that all may have some pleasure in reading the sequence straight through as a single work with a special esthetic appeal of its own. It is this distinctive feature of *Superior Poems of Our Time,* as much as its historical importance, that has evoked our own interest and led to the wish to share the work with the Western reader.

Our approach will be familiar to those who have read our *Japanese Court Poetry,* in which we attempted to adapt modern Western critical practice to an older and different poetic tradition. In that attempt we considered both explicit and implicit critical principles and sought to characterize and evaluate the literary qualities of poems normally found in anthologies and sequences. Our treatment of Teika's work is in a sense a microcosm of our larger study, and it will, we think, be more significant to the reader if he consults our earlier work. In the present instance we have generally refrained from critical analysis and evaluation of individual poems, emphasizing instead their function as parts of a larger structure. In the Introduction we have described the techniques by which Teika integrated the poems into a unified sequence, and the notes to the poems include a running commentary on the literary unity of the whole, as well as notes on the authorship, provenance, and poetic features of the poems as discrete works, and other information primarily of interest to specialists. A few of the poems in this book appeared earlier in *Japanese Court Poetry*; some of them have been retranslated or modified.

We wish to express our gratitude for generous help that has been given us both in the United States and in Japan. We thank Professor Jinichi Konishi for his warm encouragement and continued interest in our work. Professor Kashizō Mizukami has given indispensable aid in many matters, ranging from the interpretation of abstruse passages to the location of suitable illustrations. For the frontispiece and for securing permission from its anonymous owner to use it, we wish to thank Mr. Shigemi Komatsu of the Tokyo National Museum. For the portrait of Shunzei, we are indebted to the Tokyo National Museum; for the portraits of Go-Toba and Sanetomo, to the Imperial Household Library. Professor Edward G. Seidensticker kindly read our manuscript and provided valuable suggestions and criticisms. Miss Betty Smith has been the unusually keen and thorough editor of the book. The Committee on Research of the University of California, Los Angeles, and the East Asian Studies Committee of Stanford University gave support to our work in its earlier stages.

We know that countless others have gained knowledge, pleasure, and inspiration from the works of the man to whose memory this little volume is dedicated. But only we know the personal value of our many discussions with Sir George Sansom and the pleasure of our visits with him and Lady Sansom. Like the many who knew and admired him, we have our special reasons for wishing to honor his memory.

R. H. B.
E. M.

CONTENTS

Introduction   3

Superior Poems of Our Time   41

Appendix: Manuscripts and Versions of
    the Kindai Shūka   133

Glossary of Literary Terms   141

Bibliography   143

Index of First Lines   147

Index of Poets   148

FUJIWARA TEIKA'S
Superior Poems of Our Time

INTRODUCTION

When Fujiwara Teika compiled the *Kindai Shūka* (Superior Poems of Our Time) in the early thirteenth century, his main purpose was to bring together poems he regarded as models of decorum and feeling in treating the common topics of Japanese Court poetry. The collection, like the formulary rhetorics of Renaissance educators, was designed as a handbook of eminent examples to be imitated by aspiring writers. In the words of Teika's son Tameie, "One should constantly pore over the best of the poems of old, pondering them with the determination to make one's own compositions like them, and with the firm conviction that in these are to be found the best of all styles."[1]

Teika's choices of model poems often provide valuable insights into his personal tastes and literary values. An example is the old and revered *Haru tatsu to,* by Mibu no Tadamine (fl. ca. 910), which he offers as a model opening poem.[2] One of the most famous poems of the Early Classical Period, it continued to be

[1] Fujiwara Tameie, *Yakumo Kuden* (or *Eiga Ittei*), in *Nihon Kagaku Taikei* (hereafter *NKGT*), rev. ed. (Kazama Shobō, 1955), III, 395. (All works cited are published in Tokyo, unless otherwise indicated.) This treatise, believed to have been written about 1263, sets forth Tameie's conservative views, stressing the importance of practice and advocating a poetry of bland simplicity that became the ideal of the senior Nijō family of poets descended from him.

[2] *Haru tatsu to* was the opening poem of the *Shūishū*, the third imperial anthology (ca. 1000). Its inclusion in this and other early collections, notably the "unofficial" *Kokin Waka Rokujō* and Fujiwara Kintō's *Wakan Rōeishū*, guaranteed the poem's worth to poets of the Mid-Classical Period. In the twelfth and thirteenth centuries, it was quoted in Fujiwara Shunzei's

admired and imitated by poets of the Mid-Classical Period and was cited again and again in standard anthologies and treatises. Nevertheless, it is significant that Teika chose it in preference to a number of equally famous rivals. The choice of love poems perforce implies Teika's view of the importance of the Japanese literary tradition of courtly love and those of its conventions which seemed most relevant to the literary experience of his own day. In choosing for his concluding poem one by his father, Shunzei, Teika revealed his family loyalty and also, perhaps, the desire to end the sequence on a note of personal sorrow. Personal as his reasons may often have been, however, he never departed from the accepted canons of poetic taste in his time. All eighty-three poems of the *Kindai Shūka* had appeared in imperial anthologies—an indication of the esteem in which they were held by Teika's literary predecessors and contemporaries—and the *Kindai Shūka* itself was patterned on the structure of the imperial anthologies.[8]

As with many long-lived literary works, the interest of Teika's anthology has changed with time. Today its appeal is in part biographical; we value it for what it tells us of Teika, a remarkable poet, critic, and personality. The importance of the anthology to us lies in the literary merit of the poems (rather than in their utility as models for imitation), and in the techniques of association and progression by which Teika fashioned the poems into an artistic whole. For, as we shall make clear, the *Kindai Shūka* is not merely a collection, but a work of art in its own right.

Korai Fūteishō, Go-Shirakawa's *Ryōjin Hishō,* and other treatises by Teika and by his son Tameie. It was again quoted in the *Sangoki,* a fourteenth-century treatise.

[8] For a list of the twenty-one imperial anthologies compiled from the tenth century to the fifteenth, with dates of compilation, names of compilers, and other information, see Robert H. Brower and Earl Miner, *Japanese Court Poetry* (Stanford, Calif.: Stanford University Press, 1961), pp. 482–86 (hereafter *JCP*). The eighth anthology was completed shortly before the *Kindai Shūka.*

As might be expected, however, *Superior Poems of Our Time* has acquired an encrustation of problems that come between it and the modern reader. We shall take up some of them in the pages that follow, relegating discussion of the complex textual problems to the Appendix.

Teika as Poet, Critic, and Teacher

Fujiwara Teika (1162–1241) was born into a family of noblemen and poets. He was a descendant of the great Fujiwara Michinaga, who became virtual dictator of Japan at the end of the tenth century, and although the family line had come down through a succession of younger sons, Teika's forebears had held respectable positions at Court. In the preface to *Superior Poems of Our Time,* Teika writes, with a pride scarcely muted by ceremonial politeness, that he represents the third generation of a poetic house. His grandfather Toshitada was a poet of some accomplishment, and his father, Shunzei (1114–1204), was a great poet and the seminal literary thinker of his age.[4] Although Shunzei never achieved a higher Court office than that of Chamberlain to the Empress Dowager, his place in the literary world was unrivaled. He was given the highest literary honor a courtier could aspire to in 1183, when he was commissioned by ex-Emperor Go-Shirakawa to compile the seventh imperial anthology, the *Senzaishū*. But it was as a judge of poetry contests that he was most influential. Many stories have been handed down about his fairness and his willingness to appreciate the best qualities of any style or poet. He introduced positive criteria for judgment that were more constructive than the negative criticism then prevalent, and that encouraged the adoption of his own literary ideals. Even his bitterest rivals admired his skill in winning acceptance for the poetic styles he

---

[4] The Chinese characters for Shunzei's name are sometimes pronounced Toshinari. The variant form for Teika is Sadaie.

preferred: the Priest Kenshō is said to have remarked, "Lord Shunzei took the attitude that even he sometimes made mistakes, and instead of pressing a point with any great insistence, would make such comments as, 'Since everyone does it that way these days, what does it matter if the poem lacks that particular conventional element?' "⁵ There are few more attractive literary figures than Shunzei—and few writers in any age or language whose skill and influence lasted to the age of ninety. It is not hard to understand why Teika was proud of being his son.

Teika benefited from his father's envied position and prestige, but he seems to have inherited little of Shunzei's equable temperament. In his youth he struck a superior Court official with a candlestick. According to an account by Shunzei's patron, Kujō Kanezane, Teika had been taunted into losing his temper, but his privilege to attend Court was nonetheless revoked, and he was obliged to spend the year-end holidays shut up at home.⁶ It was on Shunzei's plea that he gained reinstatement in the spring of the following year.

This isolated episode did not of itself particularly damage Teika's prospects, but given his impatience and ambition, his advancement in Court rank and office seemed agonizingly slow. The late twelfth century was a period of great political and social change, instability, and strife, and the individual careers of lesser nobles like Teika were bound up in the intrigues between the great families at Court and the struggles for power between

---

⁵ Kamo no Chōmei, *Mumyōshō*, in *NKGT*, III, 303; Hisamatsu Sen'ichi and Nishio Minoru, eds., *Karonshū, Nōgakuronshū* (Iwanami Shoten, 1961) (hereafter Hisamatsu and Nishio), p. 74, in *Nihon Koten Bungaku Taikei* (hereafter *NKTBT*), Vol. LXV. For a discussion of Shunzei's poetry and esthetic ideals and the vigorous and often embittered literary rivalry of the day—especially between Shunzei's house, the Mikohidari, and another branch of the Fujiwara, the Rokujō family—see *JCP*, Chap. VI, *passim*.

⁶ The episode is recorded in the diary of Regent and Chancellor Fujiwara (Kujō) Kanezane in the first year of Bunji (1185). (See Fujiwara Kanezane, *Gyokuyō* [Naigai Insatsu Kabushiki Kaisha, 1907], III, 118.) The poem Shunzei attached to his letter to ex-Emperor Go-Shirakawa on Teika's behalf is preserved in the *Senzaishū*, XVIII: 1155.

the provincial warrior clans, the Taira and the Minamoto. Teika was a young courtier and household retainer of the great Kujō family when Minamoto Yoritomo overthrew the Taira and established Japan's first feudal government at Kamakura in 1192. He witnessed the struggle for power at Court between the Kujō, who were sympathetic to Kamakura, and the family of Koga Michichika, who had a powerful influence over the young Emperor Go-Toba and encouraged him in his growing resolve to overthrow the feudal government after his abdication in 1197. Teika was dismayed to see his own hopes for promotion dashed when Michichika ousted the Kujō from power in a political coup in 1196. As a result, Teika remained ignominiously stuck in the post of Lesser Commander of the Palace Guards of the Left (*Sakon'e no Shōshō*) from 1189 to 1202, and his advancement to the next higher rank of Acting Middle Commander (*Gon no Chūjō*) may have been largely due to Shunzei's influence with the poetically inclined, young ex-Emperor, Go-Toba. But it was not until he was over fifty that Teika's Court ranks and offices began even remotely to approach his desires and estimate of his own merit. He was seventy years old before he attained his highest office of Acting Middle Counselor (*Gon Chūnagon*) and received the unprecedented poetic honor of being the first poet to take part in compiling two imperial anthologies.

Although he relied on his father's prestige to advance his Court rank, and although he benefited from Shunzei's achievement as a poet and a critic, Teika established his literary reputation by his own talents. The distinctive literary style of his youth and early middle age was not the style of "mystery and depth" (*yūgen*) that Shunzei had made into one of the great styles and ideals of the age, but rather the style of "ethereal beauty" (*yōen*), which appears to have been particularly admired by Teika's younger contemporaries. The beauty of Teika's yōen style speaks for itself in poems like the one that opens

7

the fifth book of love poems in the eighth imperial anthology, the *Shinkokinshū*:

Shirotae no	On the white sleeves
Sode no wakare ni	Covering us until our parting,
Tsuyu ochite	Dew falls with our tears,
Mi ni shimu iro no	And the autumn wind blows in presentiment
Akikaze zo fuku.	A bleak color that penetrates the heart.

The symbolic whiteness of the autumn wind, which is first suggested by the white sleeves and the dew-tears, and allusions to two earlier poems give the poem the richness of texture that characterizes the yōen style.

Another characteristic of yōen is an almost Symbolist use of language, in which combinations of images evoke a mysterious, dreamlike atmosphere, as in this autumn poem in the *Shinkokinshū*, which has a strong element of romantic love:

Samushiro ya	On her mat of straw,
Matsu yo no aki no	The Lady of the Bridge of Uji
Kaze fukete	Spreads the moonlight out,
Tsuki o katashiku	And in the waiting autumn night
Uji no hashihime.	Still lies there in the darkening wind.

In this poem Teika uses traditional diction in startling ways. The spreading of moonlight has the ethereal beauty of the yōen style; a waiting night and a darkening wind are even more magical. That such an experience (enriched once again by allusion to older literature) should be conceived of as essentially autumnal is characteristic of Teika's intensity and, it may be said, ingenuity, of poetic conception.[7]

Teika's success in the poetry gatherings at Go-Toba's Court attracted many imitators. His achievement was recognized in 1201, when the young ex-Emperor commissioned him to help compile the eighth imperial anthology. Teika was represented

---

[7] These two poems and the older works alluded to are discussed at greater length in *JCP*, pp. 317–18 and 467, and pp. 276–77 and 454–55. On Teika and the yōen style, see *JCP*, Chap. VI, pp. 262–65 and *passim*.

in this anthology by more poems than any other poet of his generation. The early years of the thirteenth century were not, however, as auspicious for him as these honors suggest. The poetic honors brought little in the way of tangible rewards or promotions, whereas Teika's economic resources were barely adequate to provide for his growing family and household. Indeed, his expenses were increased by Go-Toba's favor, for Teika often had to follow the restless, pleasure-seeking ex-Emperor to one or another of his outlying palaces and country residences, when His Majesty let it be known that a poetry party was to be among the day's amusements. Teika had to pay all his own expenses on these excursions (they often kept him from home for days at a time), and his outlays for clothing, provisions, lodging, and transportation were considerable. He severely disapproved of the ex-Emperor's mode of life, blaming it on the stupidity and irresponsibility of his chief ministers, the political enemies of Teika and his Kujō patrons.

Further, his appointment as one of the compilers of the *Shinkokinshū* was not an unmixed blessing. His work on the anthology, carried on over an agonizingly long period, was a source of constant irritation and frustration. Teika disapproved of many of the poems chosen—often the ones picked by Go-Toba, who took an unusually active part in preparing the collection—and he felt that his own views were being slighted.[8] Teika's political and literary enemies alleged that he had made slighting remarks about the ex-Emperor's judgment, and relations between Teika and Go-Toba gradually became cool. Go-Toba was justifiably offended in 1207, when it came to his ears that Teika had been harshly and openly criticizing him for his failure to appreciate one of Teika's own poems.

[8] Nearly two years after the official completion of the *Shinkokinshū*, Teika wrote in his diary: "By command of the ex-Emperor we are cutting up the *Shinkokin* again, adding and subtracting poems at the flick of a finger. With respect to all these revisions, not a particle of attention is paid to my opinion." *Meigetsuki* (Kokusho Kankōkai, 1911), II, 47.

The causes for dissatisfaction on both sides multiplied with time. Thus, although it was a distinct material advantage as well as a high honor for Teika to be requested to become teacher of poetry to the young shogun Minamoto Sanetomo in 1209, his acceptance must have affronted Go-Toba, who regarded the feudal authorities as usurpers and was actively plotting their destruction.[9] At the same time, Go-Toba worried Teika exceedingly by encouraging his young heir Tameie to develop his natural talent for Court football, even to the point of hinting that he might substitute it for poetry as the family tradition of expertise. Something of Teika's paternal concern can be glimpsed from an entry in his diary in 1213:

I am told that these days Captain Tameie does nothing but play football day and night. . . . He never so much as glances at a book. He has even forgotten what little he knew at the age of seven or eight, when, with great difficulty, he produced his first sequence of one hundred poems. This is all due to the evil karma of our whole house; it is the punishment for having formed bad connections and piled up a burden of evil deeds in past lives. . . . My issue have been few at best—only two sons—and when I think that they cannot even write their Japanese syllabary properly, I see the extinction of our house already before my eyes.[10]

An open breach took place in 1220, when Go-Toba, offended by an implied rebuke in one of Teika's poems, barred him from all poetic functions at Court. In a poetic treatise of his own,

---

[9] Sanetomo initiated the relationship by sending Teika thirty of his best poems, composed since he was fifteen. Teika sent him letters, criticisms of his verses, and copies of anthologies, later making in his own hand a copy of a collection of Sanetomo's poems, composed before he was twenty-two, known as the *Teika-bon Kinkaishū*. When he compiled the *Shinchokusenshū*, he included twenty-five of his late disciple's poems. Among the advantages that accrued to Teika soon after forming this important connection was prompt action by the feudal authorities against an unruly steward on one of Teika's most important manors. See Maruyama Shūichi, *Fujiwara Teika*, rev. ed., 225–26.

[10] *Meigetsuki*, II, 274–75.

thought to have been written after Go-Toba had been exiled to the Oki Islands for the remainder of his life, the ex-Emperor wrote in defense of his taste and judgment in poetry, with particular reference to Teika, who now stood at the pinnacle of poetic prestige at Court. It is not surprising, especially in view of the fact that Teika had completely ignored him since his exile, that his grudging admiration for Teika's poetic powers should be mixed with asperity toward what he considered his haughtiness and intransigence:

Teika is in a class by himself. When one considers that he thought even the poems of his father, who was such a superior poet, to be shallow affairs, it should be clear that he did not consider it worth his while to bother with the poems of other people. His style of complexity of treatment combined with a gentle elegance was indeed hard to find anywhere else, and his mastery of the art was remarkable. But the way he behaved as if he knew all about poetry was really extraordinary. Especially when he was defending his own opinion, he would act like the man who insisted a stag was a horse. He was utterly oblivious of others and would exceed all reason, refusing to listen to anything other people had to say.... He would never take into consideration any extenuating circumstances of time or occasion in his judgment of a poem, and because he himself was incapable of taking a relaxed, casual attitude toward poetry, even when people would praise one of his own poems, if it happened to be one of which he was not particularly proud, he would scowl angrily.[11]

---

[11] *Go-Toba no In Gokuden*, in *NKGT*, III, 5; Hisamatsu and Nishio, p. 148. Go-Toba's astonishing statement about Teika's attitude toward the poems of Shunzei is completely unfounded. If, as may have been the case, the ex-Emperor wrote his treatise after Teika compiled the *Shinchokusenshū* in 1234, such a malicious remark may be understandable: not a single one of Go-Toba's poems was included in this ninth imperial anthology, and his anger and disappointment must have been extreme. Go-Toba may also have looked back upon Teika's connection with Sanetomo as a kind of treason, as the comparison of Teika to the man who insisted a stag was a horse perhaps suggests. Go-Toba alludes to the Chinese *Historical Records* (Shih Chi), where it is written that Chao Kao (d. 207 B.C.), plotting to overthrow the Emperor, brought him a stag, claiming it was a horse. The Emperor laughed, but some of the courtiers took Chao Kao's part and insisted it was indeed a horse. Thus Chao Kao knew that the courtiers were more afraid of him than of the Emperor, and determined to revolt.

Shunzei died in 1204. The event seems to have shaken Teika, although he was already forty-two years old; and even though he inherited his father's position as the Court's arbiter of poetic taste, throughout his forties he suffered from an inner turmoil that frustrated his creative powers. His feelings of isolation and loss were increased by the sudden death in 1206 of his chief patron, the talented young Kujō Yoshitsune, and the death of Yoshitsune's father, Kanezane, in 1207. In the Prefatory Essay to *Superior Poems of Our Time,* written when he was forty-seven, he laments that he has "forgotten the color of the flowers of words; the wellsprings of inspiration have run dry." His literary output declined markedly. The reasons for this were many. Bad health and general debility were important factors: despite a strong constitution that enabled him to live to an unusually advanced age, Teika was almost constantly ill. As a youth he had two nearly fatal illnesses that permanently weakened his health. His most persistent ailment during his middle years was a severe bronchial condition, which tortured him with a racking cough and made him susceptible to an endless series of colds. In the autumn of 1208, the year before he compiled the first version of the *Kindai Shūka,* he had a seizure while riding in his carriage; he arrived home half-conscious and remained seriously ill for several days.

There was also the emotional effect of his father's death so quickly followed by those of Yoshitsune and Kanezane. Moreover, in the earlier part of this period his duties as a compiler of the *Shinkokinshū* left little leisure for his own poetry, and in the later part the ex-Emperor's flagging interest led to a decline in the number of poetry parties and contests at Court, so that there was far less demand for formal poetry. Basically, however, Teika appears to have felt a loss of inspiration, and poetry became, for a time, a sad burden. When he was fifty years old, he wrote in his diary, "Since entering on old age it has been intolerably difficult to compose poems," and, in the same year,

"Now that I am old my poetic style has become exhausted—not one of my poems is up to standard."[12]

Gradually, Teika regained his creative powers. During his period of depression he developed a new stylistic ideal: *ushin,* or "conviction of feeling," which is both a distinct style and a requisite for all good poetry.[13] Yōen no longer claimed his deepest admiration; he did not even list it as one of the ten possible poetic styles in the *Maigetsushō* (Monthly Notes; 1219?), his most detailed treatise. Teika's sensibility was now no less acute, but the experience of his forties appears to have taught him to prefer a hard-won integrity of tone. The conviction of feeling he prized, and its frequent simplicity of expression, can best be shown by a love poem he composed when he was seventy:

Hajime yori	Although I had heard
Au wa wakare to	From the beginning that to meet
Kikinagara	Can only mean to part,
Akatsuki shirade	I gave myself to love for you
Hito o koikeri.	Unconscious of the coming dawn.

Lovers part in this poem, as in the earlier poem in the yōen style, but there is no longer an autumn wind to blow its color into their hearts. Maturity of language has replaced the dazzling virtuosity of the earlier style; remote beauty has yielded to greater immediacy.[14] In his mature years Teika was able to convey a youthful intensity of passion all the stronger and purer for his having denied himself some of his earlier resources.

It was also during his forties, when his characteristic style began to change, that he was increasingly called upon to teach others who wished to follow the "way" of poetry. We may well believe that the task of teaching ambitious young men to com-

---

[12] *Meigetsuki,* II, 183, 215.

[13] See *JCP,* pp. 258–59 and 270–71, for a discussion of Teika's late stylistic ideals.

[14] The poem is from a sequence composed in 1232, and is included in the *Shokushūishū* (XIII: 927), the twelfth imperial anthology.

Introduction

pose poetry contributed to the distress of this unhappy decade, but it also produced several important and peculiarly Japanese pieces of literary criticism. Among the most famous of these treatises are the Prefatory Essay to *Superior Poems of Our Time*, which Teika wrote for the young shogun Minamoto Sanetomo, and the longer and more important *Maigetsushō*, which may also have been addressed to Sanetomo.[15]

Sanetomo was a talented youth with many problems besides learning the art of poetry. The Priest Eisai, who was instrumental in introducing the cult of tea to Japan, vainly tried to help Sanetomo overcome alcoholism by weaning him from liquor to tea. The shogun's short, unhappy life, haunted by political intrigue, ended with his assassination by a nephew.[16] The poetic problems of Sanetomo are to be found in his self-conscious poetry, and in his attempt to broach the prevailing literary stan-

---

15 The *Maigetsushō* is in the form of a letter to a young pupil who had sent to Teika for correction his monthly set of one hundred poems. One family of manuscripts preserves a colophon, signed by Tameie, stating that the letter was sent "to someone" on the second day of the seventh month of the first year of Jōkyū (1219), but the original colophon in Tameie's hand is not extant, and its authenticity has been questioned. The identity of the recipient is also uncertain, with one tradition, stemming from a passage in Ton'a's *Seiashō*, holding that it was the "Kinugasa Great Inner Minister" Fujiwara Ieyoshi, and another, deriving from a statement by Shōtetsu in *Tesshoki Monogatari*, that it was Sanetomo. (See *Seiashō*, in *NKGT*, V, 23; and *Tesshoki Monogatari*, in *ibid.*, p. 233, or Hisamatsu and Nishio, p. 186.) Sanetomo was assassinated in the first month of 1219, so if the date given in Tameie's colophon is correct, the letter could hardly have been addressed to him. However, much of the advice in the letter seems so appropriate to Sanetomo from what we know of his poetry, that we are strongly inclined to side with those who question the colophon and feel that the letter must, indeed, have been intended for him. Relevant passages are translated in *JCP*, pp. 246–47 and 258–59.

16 Cf. Wm. Theodore de Bary, et al., eds., *Sources of Japanese Tradition* (New York: Columbia University Press, 1958), p. 263. Sanetomo was never more than the nominal shogun; he was a puppet in the hands of his ruthless mother, Hōjō Masako, and her family. An attempt to depose him was made as early as 1205 by his grandfather Hōjō Tokimasa. The attempt was unsuccessful, but Sanetomo thereafter lived in constant fear for his life. He wrote most of his poetry between the ages of seventeen and twenty-two, and then sank steadily into inactivity and despair.

14

dards of his day. In a bold but ill-fated departure from accepted canons, he adopted a vigorous style inspired by a handful of poems in the *Man'yōshū* (ca. 759), the great early collection that preceded the imperial anthologies. Modern Japanese poets and critics have extravagantly admired both Sanetomo and his poetry (scarcely bothering to distinguish between the two), but the more detached observer must admit that Sanetomo's achievement fell far short of his ideal. His chief defects are sentimentality, an often absurdly archaic style, and lack of poetic control. Japanese Court poetry is remarkable for its lack of sentimentality, and Teika's insistence upon conviction of feeling as the essence of all poetic styles should have discouraged Sanetomo's emotional self-indulgence. Moreover, Teika's most explicit advice in the *Maigetsushō* is that a novice "not permit himself to become enamored of the archaic style." The same point is made more subtly in the Prefatory Essay to *Superior Poems of Our Time*.

To teach Sanetomo what was central to Japanese poetry and to inculcate artistic control, Teika turned to the method of teaching by example, a method practiced for centuries in China and Japan by master artists. The theory behind the practice is very simple: one learns by doing, and one learns to do well by imitating the achievements of the great. The master set the example by selecting poems to be imitated or by letting the disciple observe him in the studio or theater. In poetry this approach can best be called exemplary or formulary criticism, as the titles of anthologies compiled by Teika show: *Nishidaishū* (Collection of Twice Four Eras); *Eiga Taigai* (Essentials of Poetic Composition); *Shūka no Daitai* (A Basic Canon of Superior Poems); *Hyakunin Shūka* (Superior Poems by One Hundred Poets); *Hyakunin Isshu* (Single Poems by One Hundred Poets); and *Hachidaishū Shūitsu* (Best Poems from the Anthologies of Eight Eras).[17]

17 For a description of the above titles, see the Bibliography, pp. 145–46.

These formulary collections are distillations of other collections, especially the imperial anthologies. The poems are those thought most worthy of imitation for their diction, imagery, decorum, or overall style. It was left to the disciple to discover just what features of these poems should be considered exemplary. Having thoroughly studied these models, the student composed a sheaf of poems and submitted it to the master for judgment. The master simply marked—with a circle, a check, or one of the similar marks still used by teachers in Japan—those poems which showed that the disciple had learned his lesson. Again the student was left to infer what he had done right, until by constant study, reflection, and practice he made the standards of the masters his own.

The Prefatory Essay

The Prefatory Essay, in the version we have translated, opens with the sentence "This is now a thing of the distant past"— a sentence Teika added when he returned to the essay several years after its first writing.[18] The rest of the brief preamble is a conventional self-deprecatory statement. The essay itself begins with a description of the history of Japanese poetry from the writers in the *Kokinshū* (ca. 905), the first imperial anthology, to Teika's own day. Teika praises Ki no Tsurayuki, the chief compiler of the *Kokinshū* and author of its famous Japanese Preface (the first extended critical essay in Japanese), for composing poems with literary virtues that writers in subsequent ages could not equal, though he seriously qualifies his praise by adding that Tsurayuki did not compose "in the style of overtones and ethereal beauty." But despite the degeneration since

---

[18] There are two "versions" of the *Kindai Shūka*. The first, sent to Sanetomo, is traditionally known as the "version sent away." The later version— the one we have translated—is called the "holograph." The two versions differ on several points, as will be explained below, and unless the version sent away is specifically mentioned, the title *Kindai Shūka* is used here to mean the holograph.

Tsurayuki's time, a few poets—those whose poems are in the version sent away—have departed from the vulgar poetic styles of these later ages and have sought to recapture the ancient styles. The achievement of these exceptional modern poets has been to recover the "proper style of poetry" (*sama*), established by Tsurayuki as the standard by which innovations were measured, and practiced before him in the period of the so-called Six Poetic Geniuses or *Rokkasen* (830–90), especially by Bishop Henjō, Ariwara Narihira, and Ono no Komachi. Although these poets are well represented in the *Kokinshū*, their poetry flourished a generation or two earlier. Teika argues in this oblique fashion that the good poetry of recent times is not a novel departure, as some foolish young writers think.[19]

Notwithstanding the fact that Teika found Tsurayuki's poetic styles inadequate in certain respects, many of the nuances of his essay style can only be fully appreciated by recalling the Japanese Preface to the *Kokinshū*. In this beautiful and witty essay, Tsurayuki had criticized the Six Poetic Geniuses and given his praise to still earlier poets whose works appear in the *Man'yōshū*. Teika borrows this pattern of historical judgment, and even adapts some of Tsurayuki's most famous phrasing. In comparing some recent poetry to the country bumpkin who has left "the shelter of the blossoms," he is echoing Tsurayuki's criticism of the poet Ōtomo Kuronushi for being "like a mountaineer with a load of wood on his back stopping to rest under the cherry blossoms." When he says that degenerate modern poetry can be compared to "the merchant taking off his gor-

---

[19] In a dialogue by Kamo no Chōmei, one of the most original poets among Teika's contemporaries, two men discuss the "style of recent times" (yūgen). One asks whether it is really true, as some hostile critics allege, that this modern style is totally new. The other replies that literary styles are bound to change but that the modern style has not been conjured up out of thin air: "This is a criticism made by those who do not have a thorough familiarity with the *Kokinshū*. In that anthology there are all manner of poetic styles, . . . including this style of mystery and depth." *Mumyōshō*, in *NKGT*, III, 310; Hisamatsu and Nishio, p. 84.

geous robes," he is adapting Tsurayuki's description of Bunya Yasuhide as a "vulgar merchant dressing himself up in fine clothes."

Some of Teika's most touching remarks are those expressing admiration for his father and revealing his own unease of mind. Shunzei, he says, had told him that poetry "proceeds from the heart"—a phrase that recalls Tsurayuki's famous statement that Japanese poetry has its roots in the human heart. When Teika says that he has been "spoken of with scorn," he is referring in part to the criticism that had been leveled against his yōen style. Certain poets had unwittingly parodied this style, writing verses that the age scorned as "Daruma poems" because they sounded like the gibberish of Zen priests, and yōen had come into disfavor.[20] Teika complains that he is old, ill, and out of tune with writing, having "forgotten what little I once knew."

Much of the essay is marked by the prescriptive element characteristic of so much Japanese criticism in this period. For example, Teika limits the amount of another's poem that may be incorporated into one's own verses and sharply distinguishes between "old words," the poetic diction and phrasing inherited from the past, which young poets may well use, and "words that belong to others," that is, words that have been removed from the public domain because of their use in famous poems. For "old words," Teika advocates using the poetic language established by the first three imperial anthologies. These seemingly trivial matters are related to central concerns of Shunzei and

---

[20] Teika's style of ethereal beauty was attacked by the Rokujō family, which was desperately trying to overthrow the Mikohidari in both poetry and politics. Teika was deeply discouraged for a time, but Go-Toba's patronage helped pull him out of this early slump. Many years later he wrote, "In the Bunji [1185–89] and Kenkyū [1190–98] eras, I was slandered by everyone in the world, high and low, for what they called my 'new-fangled style,' my 'incomprehensible Daruma verses,' until I wanted to abandon poetry entirely. But then in the Shōji [1199–1200] and Kennin [1201–3] eras, ... in response to the august favor of the Sage Ex-Sovereign and his Sacred Rule, albeit I did no more than carry on the traditions of my house, I took up this art once again." *Shūi Gusō Ingai*, in Reizei Tameomi, ed., *Fujiwara Teika Zenkashū* (Bummeisha, 1940), p. 376.

Teika. The specification of what may and what may not be used from the past is designed to show Sanetomo how to apply Teika's conservative ideal of diction. Teika links this ideal to others he considers equally important: originality of treatment, a striving for the serious and elevated, and emulation of the emotional intensity of the Six Poetic Geniuses.

The modesty of the conclusion is more than convention. His knowledge "differs in no respect from what has been recorded by various people," Teika says, invoking traditional support for his view that such aberrations as Sanetomo's taste for the "archaic style" of the *Man'yōshū* cannot be conducive to good verse. Sanetomo, who was not old enough to qualify for strong opinions, had been warned against such follies earlier in the essay by Teika's remark that "students of the art among the younger generation today appear sincerely to think that they are composing real poetry while actually they know nothing about its proper style . . . perhaps because it has become universal for people to choose the most inappropriate poems as models." Sanetomo may not have understood that his admiration for the poems of the *Man'yōshū* placed him among the sincere and misguided, but Teika was not thinking only of him. Other young poets misunderstood the proper styles of poetry and made a "fetish" of obscurity, "changing what ought to be simple into something difficult, yoking together things that have no relation to one another."[21]

---

[21] An astute evaluation of the young poetic imitators of the day is to be found in the dialogue by Chōmei mentioned in note 19. Chōmei's alter ego says, "How painful it is to witness the ridiculous attempts of those without adequate styles of their own, who have not yet reached the summit of the mountain and who yet insist on trying to imitate the style by guesswork. It is as if some low-born country wench, knowing that it is the genteel thing to use cosmetics, were to smear all sorts of things on her face, just as her ignorant fancy dictated. Such people never invent things for themselves, but merely imitate the styles of other people by gathering up for their own use all their discarded tags and phrases. Such expressions as, 'the dew grows old,' 'the wind grows late,' 'the inner fastnesses of the heart,' 'the bottom of pathos,' 'the sky at dawn of the moon,' 'the dusk of wind,' 'my native

Teika's essay is not an anatomy of poetry; it relies upon examples and ideals rather than critical terminology and analysis. In these respects it is typical both of its age and of a major strain of Japanese poetic criticism. Some two hundred years later Imagawa Ryōshun wrote, "There is no text that gives a better understanding of poetry than the epistle presented to Sanetomo of Kamakura by Lord Teika."[22] In its brevity and deftness, Teika's essay reveals the hand of a poet, the same sure hand that made a little anthology of eighty-three poems a consummate work of art.

The Exemplary Poems

Thirty-seven known poets are represented in the *Kindai Shūka,* nineteen of them by a single poem, the others by two or more. There are ten anonymous poems. All the poems are in the form of the *tanka* or "short poem," which consists of thirty-one syllables grouped in five lines: five syllables in the first and third lines and seven in the others. Teika's immediate source for the eighty-three poems was probably his *Nishidaishū,* a larger collection compiled in 1215 from the first eight imperial anthologies. Teika's knowledge of the oldest poems' authorship depended on ascriptions in his ultimate sources, the imperial anthologies. According to these sources, the oldest poem in the sequence (15) is attributed, with dubious validity, to Emperor Tenchi (626–71). Next in order of age are three poems (19, 50,

---

village of spring'—these may well have sounded fresh and unusual when they were first employed in a poem, but to use them over again is simply to imitate a handful of trifling mannerisms. Sometimes people try to give the impression that they have some deep though vague and confused feeling to express, only to find in the end that they have produced a verse which makes no sense at all, even to themselves. Poems of this stamp have nothing to do with mystery and depth. They may justly be called the gibberish of the Daruma sect." *Mumyōshō,* in *NKGT,* III, 311–12; Hisamatsu and Nishio, p. 86.

22 See Kojima Yoshio and Tanaka Hiroshi, *"Kindai Shūka,"* in *Gunsho Kaidai,* IX (Zoku Gunsho Ruijū Kanseikai, 1960), 131. Ryōshun was the pupil of Teika's great-grandson Reizei Tamehide, and was one of the most important critics of the late fourteenth century.

さうやまさ迎きにれ小ーせうろか
らうのふみちあそけあまくり
村
山中小みちゝゝ
山中小みちゝゝあきれふいつしう
やまれふくくにししそなくくなる

Fujiwara Shunzei, from the *Jidai Fudō Utaawase* (Contest of Poems from Different Ages), an illustrated scroll of the Kamakura period (thirteenth century). To the right of the figure, Yukihira's poem on the Imperial Excursion to Saga (no. 75, pp. 122–23 below) is matched with Shunzei's famous lament (no. 83, pp. 130–31).

Ex-Emperor Go-Toba (above) and Minamoto Sanetomo (below), from the *Tennō Sekkan Daijin Ei* (Portraits of Emperors, Regents, Chancellors, and Great Ministers), Kamakura period.

64) that are traditionally, but quite as questionably, attributed to the great Kakinomoto Hitomaro (fl. ca. 680–710); poem 19 even appears in the *Man'yōshū* in a slightly different version and among a group of anonymous poems.[23]

The largest group of poems in the sequence, including all the anonymous poems, is from the Early Classical Period (784–1100)—more specifically from the period covered by the first three imperial anthologies, the *Kokinshū, Gosenshū,* and *Shūishū,* or roughly the years 830 to 1000. It is the inclusion of so very many early poems that makes the traditional title, *Superior Poems of Our Time,* a misleading name for Teika's sequence. The latter part of the ninth century, roughly the Age of the Six Poetic Geniuses (called in the Prefatory Essay the Kampei era), is represented by eleven poems of five poets: Ono no Komachi (6); Sarumaru Dayū (20); Bishop Henjō (30, 31, 77); Priest Sosei (4, 62, 82); and Ariwara Yukihira (36, 37, 75). However, most of the poems from the Early Classical Period are by poets who were active in the tenth century. The first half of the century—what might be called the Age of the *Kokinshū* or the Age of Tsurayuki—is represented by ten poets with sixteen poems: one poem each by Ki no Tsurayuki (21), Ki no Tomonori (7), Fujiwara Toshiyuki (66), Ōe no Chisato (11), Bunya Asayasu (16), and Kiyowara Fukayabu (8); two poems each by Mibu no Tadamine (1, 59), Minamoto Hitoshi (43, 44), and Sakanoue Korenori (27, 56); and four poems by Lady Ise (47, 49, 69, 70). The second half of the century, sometimes designated the Age of the *Shūishū* or the Age of Kintō (Fujiwara Kintō was the most influential critic of his day and the compiler of the *Shūishū*), is represented by eight poets and ten poems: one each by Minamoto Saneakira (22), Fujiwara Koretada (52), Sone no Yoshitada (51), Kiyowara Motosuke (68), Fujiwara Michinobu

---

[23] Citations of poems from the *Man'yōshū* and the imperial anthologies, as well as other sources, significant variants, dates of poets, and the like, are given in the notes to the individual poems below.

(33), and Lady Izumi Shikibu (32); two each by Prince Moto-
naga (63, 65) and Priest Egyō or Ekei (9, 25).

The eleventh century, often called the Age of the *Goshūishū*
(after the fourth imperial anthology), is represented only by
Lady Kii (54). Teika seems to be thinking mainly of the age of
the *Goshūishū* when in his Prefatory Essay he deplores intellec-
tual inferiority and vulgar diction.[24] With the late eleventh cen-
tury began the period Teika calls the "recent past" or "modern
times." Minamoto Tsunenobu (1016–97; poems 18, 29, 76) is
the oldest modern poet mentioned in the Prefatory Essay and
the great exception to the general rule of mediocrity in the
eleventh century; his descriptive poetry and "lofty style" did
much to keep serious poetry alive in an age of bland versifying
and witless witticisms.

Seven more poets of the "recent past," together with three of
Teika's own generation, complete the sequence. The seven in-
clude the chief representatives of both the innovating and the
conservative poetic factions; all but Chancellor Fujiwara Tada-
michi (13) were what might be called professional poets, and
except for Tadamichi and Saigyō, all had been included in the
version sent away. Tsunenobu's son Minamoto Shunrai, a lead-
ing innovator of the early twelfth century, is represented by
four poems (2, 41, 48, 57); his arch rival, the scholar and conser-
vative critic Fujiwara Mototoshi, by but one (78). The two major
poets of the Rokujō house are also included: Akisuke (53) and
Kiyosuke (24, 79). However, these conservative poets are not so
well represented here as they were in the collection sent to Sane-
tomo. Finally, Teika selects five poems by the great Priest Saigyō
(10, 23, 35, 73, 74), and six poems—more than by any other poet
—by his father, Shunzei (38, 39, 45, 58, 80, 83).[25] The three con-

---

24 Shunzei also criticized the degenerate poetry of the eleventh century as
represented in the *Goshūishū*: "Owing perhaps to the personal tastes of the
compiler, the poems are mostly in the 'witty style.' . . . In comparison with
the various other anthologies, they are considerably less elevated in tone and
conception." *Korai Fūteishō*, in *NKGT*, II, 313–14.

25 The version sent away included twenty-seven poems by six poets: two

22

temporary poets are Fujiwara (Kujō) Yoshitsune (28, 42), Fuji-
wara Ietaka (40, 72), and ex-Emperor Go-Toba (3, 12, 34, 71).
Although Teika doubtless chose the poems for themselves rather
than their authors, it is interesting to note that all three men
had significantly influenced his life: Yoshitsune and Go-Toba
had been his patrons, and Ietaka was his close friend, a leading
disciple of Shunzei, the son-in-law of Shunzei's adopted son,
Jakuren, and a fellow-compiler of the *Shinkokinshū*.

Thus most of the poems in the *Kindai Shūka* are derived
from two periods: the Age of the *Sandaishū* or first three impe-
rial anthologies, and the "recent past," including Teika's con-
temporaries. The emphasis reveals Teika's taste and training,
as well as the standards he hoped to inculcate in his pupils, and
it conforms with the opinions on the history of Japanese poetry
set forth in his Prefatory Essay. A preference for these two great
ages of Japanese poetry—explicit in the Prefatory Essay and
implicit in the selection of poems—appears in much of Teika's
criticism; it reflects Shunzei's dictum that the fundamentals of
poetic style were to be sought in the *Kokinshū*.[26]

Although both Shunzei and Teika had an unusual interest in
the poetry of the Early Literary Period and advocated study of
its great anthology, it can be seen that it was not from the *Man'-
yōshū* that Teika chose his exemplary poems for the *Kindai
Shūka*. True, the poems attributed to Tenchi and Hitomaro
were believed to derive from the Early Literary Period, but in
conception they are more typical of the Early Classical Period.
Two of these poems (15 and 19) are examples of an elegant pas-
toralism more representative of later, romanticized pictures of
the early literary age than of the age itself. The two other very
old poems (50 and 64) exemplify the use of two rhetorical tech-
niques—the *kakekotoba* or pivot-word, and the *jokotoba* or
semi-metaphorical "preface"—that had been especially prized

---

by Mototoshi, three each by Tsunenobu and Akisuke, four by Kiyosuke,
seven by Shunzei, and eight by Shunrai.
[26] *Korai Fūteishō*, in *NKGT*, II, 312.

Teika's holograph.
The first page of poems from the *Kindai Shūka*.

in the Early Classical Period, and that had, by Teika's time, long since become skills to be mastered by every young poet.

In assessing the significance of Teika's choices on other than historical grounds, one is faced with numerous questions of subjective judgment. Two matters must be borne in mind in trying to derive an implicit esthetic from the poems of the *Kindai Shūka*. First, they were undoubtedly intended for a young pupil, and Teika's choice of poems was governed in part by what he thought most important for a beginning student to learn. Second, as we show in the following section, Teika shaped the poems into a coherent whole, linking them by techniques of association and progression. His choice of certain poems and rejection of others may, therefore, have been influenced by the requirements of the sequence form; that is, a given poem may have been chosen primarily for its possibilities for association in this particular sequence over other poems Teika may have admired equally.

Even though it cannot be assumed that the *Kindai Shūka* represents the unalloyed essence of Teika's personal taste, the eighty-three poems of the holograph do indeed represent what he considered, at that period of his life, the finest or most exemplary poems of the two ages he most admired. He used many of the same poems again and again in succeeding anthologies. Six poems of the *Kindai Shūka* are also in the *Shūka no Daitai,* twenty-eight in the *Hyakunin Isshu,* and forty-eight in the *Hachidaishū Shūitsu.* The poem ascribed to Emperor Tenchi (15) appears in all of these, as well as in the *Eiga Taigai* and another work, probably by Teika, known as *Teika Jittei* (Teika's Ten Styles). Only five of the eighty-three poems of the *Kindai Shūka* are unique to this one of Teika's many short anthologies and treatises. Clearly, Teika valued most of the poems for their intrinsic merit over and above their appropriateness as models for a novice or their suitability for the sequence.

On the whole, the poems of the *Kindai Shūka* are plainer,

more muted, less flamboyant or romantic, than many other famous poems from the same periods and by the same poets. It is no surprise to find Mibu no Tadamine's *Haru tatsu to,* on the coming of spring at Yoshino, beginning the sequence; this poem had been held in great respect for over three hundred years and was cited in Fujiwara Kintō's treatise *Kuhon Waka* as an example of the best of the nine classes of Japanese poetry, having a style in which "the diction is of marvelous beauty and there is even more meaning than is expressed."[27]

Haru tatsu to	Is it just because
Iu bakari ni ya	They say this is the day which marks
Mi-Yoshino no	The coming of the spring
Yama mo kasumite	That even the mountains of fair Yoshino
Kesa wa miyu ran.	Are veiled this morning in a haze?

Much of the poem's beauty lies in its lovely sound patterns and cadences: light end-pauses in lines 1 and 4, a heavier end-pause in line 2, and repeated "a" sounds in the first two lines echoed in the last two. Such beauty of sound and rhythm, together with an elegant subjectivity of conception, no doubt account in large part for the poem's enduring fame. No one could quarrel with Teika for choosing it as an opening poem, but it is significant that he chose it in preference, say, to the equally famous poem, "composed when the first day of spring fell in the old year," by Ariwara Motokata, which opens both the *Kokinshū* and Teika's own *Nishidaishū*:

Toshi no uchi ni	The Old Year not yet gone,
Haru wa kinikeri	The longed-for spring has come at last
Hitotose o	And brought confusion—
Kozo to ya iwan	For are we now to say "last year,"
Kotoshi to ya iwan.	Or should we rather say "this year"?

Motokata's cleverness, witty paradox, and pose of elegant confusion were extravagantly admired by an age enthusiastically

---

[27] Fujiwara Kintō, *Kuhon Waka,* in *NKGT,* I, 67. An annotated text of this short treatise, also known as *Waka Kuhon,* appears in Hisamatsu and Nishio, pp. 32–34.

adapting to Japanese poetry the conceits, artifices, and intellectual posturings of the Chinese "oblique" (*i-p'ang*) style of the Six Dynasties period.[28] The reputation of Motokata's poem endured; indeed, in his Prefatory Essay, Teika mentions it as one of several poems whose first two lines are too famous to be used for allusive variation. But for his first exemplary poem he chose Tadamine's instead, a poem in which wit is tempered by the description of a lovely scene and by the cadences of the language itself. In Tadamine's poem reasoning and wit are employed in the service of a fanciful conception, but they are less obtrusive, less farfetched, less baroque, than Motokata's. Tadamine's poem must have seemed to Teika, as it does to us, the more satisfying of the two, the more representative of the finer poetry of its age and thus the more suitable as a model—the more imbued, in short, with "conviction of feeling."

The poems by Teika's contemporaries and by poets from the recent past are also less ornate than many others he might have chosen. They are wholly representative of their age, they are all among its most famous poems, and yet none of them display the dazzlingly unconventional language, the romantic, ethereal beauty of Teika's own poem on the Lady of the Bridge of Uji. Again the choice of poems shows that Teika's taste is no longer the high romanticism of his youth. This alteration in taste may explain, for example, Teika's selection of Chancellor Tadamichi's poem (13), a rather bland descriptive verse with none of the shimmering overtones associated with yōen and yūgen. Though it is possible that Tadamichi's poem was included for the sake of effective progression in the sequence, it is more likely that at this period of his life Teika recognized a desirable integrity, a conviction of feeling, in this poem written in the "style of describing things as one sees them."[29]

[28] See *JCP*, pp. 168–70.
[29] The "style of describing things as one sees them" (*ken'yō*) is one of the ten styles distinguished in Teika's *Maigetsushō*.

This altered preference, which can perhaps be fully appreci-
ated only when one is aware of Teika's many alternatives, also
affected the *Nishidaishū*, the basis for most of the formularies
Teika produced in later life. Teika's new taste may owe some-
thing to his study and appreciation, in his later years, of the
Chinese poetry of the Sung dynasty, with its ideal of an inner
richness concealed by surface plainness. In a more personal
sense, it may represent a modification, though not a rejection,
of youthful enthusiasms by the mature poet—an increased ap-
preciation of emotional integrity. Of course there are many
poems in the *Kindai Shūka* full of art and artifice, but the pre-
dominance of declarative and descriptive poetry reflects Teika's
later preference for plainer styles, and gives the sequence integ-
rity and conviction of tone.

The Sequence as an Integrated Whole

The collection of poems sent to Sanetomo and the later *Kin-
dai Shūka* differ significantly in format. The poems sent to Sane-
tomo, which were relatively recent, are grouped by author. Tei-
ka comments on single poems or groups of poems and appends
a few sentences at the end. Some of the poems are given special
praise, but there appears to be no principle of order within the
six author groups: there is no subject grouping as there would
be in an imperial anthology, and no ranking of poems in order
of excellence. Nor are the poems linked by association and pro-
gression. The collection opens with an autumn poem, followed
by two congratulatory poems, followed, in turn, by a spring
poem. Each poem was selected because of its superiority or its
representativeness, but on the whole the arrangement has a
casual air. The later sequence of eighty-three poems, by con-
trast, is arranged on the pattern of an imperial anthology, with
the poems grouped by topic. Teika omitted the poets' names
and the headnotes, and added no comments on the poems.
Poems by the same author are not grouped together. Sixteen

of the twenty-seven poems sent to Sanetomo (including all three of Tsunenobu's and six of Shunzei's seven) are dispersed throughout the later sequence. Teika did not include any of his own poems in the *Kindai Shūka,* which may be explained by conventional modesty. A more surprising omission is that of Ariwara Narihira—a poet of the Early Classical Period and one of the greatest of all the Court poets—whose most famous poem Teika quotes in the Prefatory Essay. Had the *Kindai Shūka* been designed simply as a collection of model poems, Narihira surely would have been included. The anthology of eighty-three poems, however, differed in genre and purpose, and hence in principles of selection, from the version sent to Sanetomo.

The genre to which the *Kindai Shūka* belongs is the integrated poetic sequence, an artistic form that gained recognition with the compilation of the *Kokinshū.* There was one major difference in Teika's principles of selection: compilers of imperial anthologies usually avoided poems that had appeared in earlier imperial anthologies. Teika by contrast, chose only such poems. Another model for Teika's *Kindai Shūka* was the integrated sequence that a poet compiled from his own work. There was no fixed number of poems for these sequences, but a hundred-poem sequence (*hyakushuuta*) was most common. Teika's reason for choosing an odd number like eighty-three is obscure.[30] His purpose in putting together the version sent away was simply to present model poems, and this probably remained his express motive for the later, expanded collection. But the choice of the imperial anthology as his model compelled Teika to arrange his poems in a way that related them to one another. He had had a good deal of practice in ordering poems according to such principles: first, in arranging many sequences of his own poems; second, and more important, in editing the *Shinkokinshū.* The *Shinkokinshū* was the apogee of a long and com-

[30] Teika often chose an oddly unaccountable number: 103 for the *Eiga Taigai,* 101 for the *Hyakunin Shūka,* 112 for the *Shūka no Daitai.*

plex esthetic development. It is considered the greatest of the imperial anthologies after the *Kokinshū,* and its nearly two thousand poems are integrated by techniques unsurpassed in skill or beauty.[31] The lasting impression made on Teika by his work on this great anthology can be seen first in his *Nishidaishū,* an integrated sequence of 1,811 poems, and then in the *Kindai Shūka.*

The integration of the *Kindai Shūka* is achieved by the techniques of progression and association: temporal and spatial progression through subgroups in the sequence, and association of poems with related diction, images, rhetorical techniques, or motifs. Both progression and association are "paced." For example, a spatial progression is sometimes temporarily suspended, and associations are at times simple and close, at other times complex and distant. The major progressions are further interwoven with numerous subprogressions. A geographical spatial progression may be accompanied for part of its movement by an in-and-out-of-doors subprogression, or a temporal progression of the seasons by a subprogression of the hours of the day and night. The use of these integrating techniques makes possible an artistic achievement otherwise beyond the anthologist's reach. It allows Teika to create a beautiful work of art even though he is the author of none of its parts. And it is one of the means the Japanese have found to make substantial works out of their brief literary forms. The *Kindai Shūka* is therefore not only, or even preeminently, an anthology of so many poets and poems, but a poetic whole of 415 lines, in 83 stanzas.

31 For the most complete history of the development of integrating techniques and an analysis of their use, see Konishi Jin'ichi, "Association and Progression: Principles of Integration in Anthologies and Sequences of Japanese Court Poetry, A.D. 900–1350," *Harvard Journal of Asiatic Studies,* XXI (December 1958), 67–127. Cf. a later account, with other examples and analysis, in *JCP,* pp. 319–29 and 403–13. Teika's principles of integration in the *Nishidaishū* are briefly discussed in Higuchi Yoshimaro, ed., *Teika Hachidaishō to Kenkyū* (Toyohashi: Mikan Kokubun Shiryō Kankōkai, 1956–57), III, 89–96.

Since the topical divisions of the *Kindai Shūka* are the same as larger divisions of the imperial anthologies, Teika's sequence may be seen as a structural microcosm of the books and groups of books in the imperial collections:

Seasonal poems, 28 (1–28)	Love poems, 34 (41–74)
Spring, 7 (1–7)	Poems on mixed topics, 9 (75–83)
Summer, 1 (8)	Congratulatory, 3 (75–77)
Autumn, 14 (9–22)	Personal grievances, 3 (78–80)
Winter, 6 (23–28)	Autumn, 1 (81)
Congratulatory poem, 1 (29)	Buddhism, 1 (82)
Laments, 6 (30–35)	Personal grievances, 1 (83)
Parting poem, 1 (36)	
Travel poems, 4 (37–40)	

Like the imperial anthologies, the *Kindai Shūka* has two main groups of poems—seasonal poems, which open the sequence, and love poems, which begin the second half. The emphases implicit in the structure give the sequence its thematic integrity and tonal movement. The main emphasis is on life's sadness. There are more poems on the tonally dark season of autumn than on the other seasons combined, and more than twice as many on autumn and winter as on spring and summer. Following the seasonal poems is a congratulatory poem, which lends a sense of the auspicious, but this is followed by laments, a parting poem, and travel poems whose sadness has even greater human immediacy than the autumn poems. The congratulatory poems (29 and 75–77) serve to mark off major divisions and to relieve the prevailing darkness of the sequence with a momentary brightness.

In the second half of the sequence, the sadness of human life gains increasing emphasis. By Teika's time, the treatment of courtly love had become as conventional in Japan as it became in Europe. The best-established convention was the unhappy dénouement, unhappy especially from the woman's point of view. The darkening of tone does not, however, preclude the celebration of beauty—in fact, it is the harmonizing of these two tonal motifs that marks this sequence, as it does so much Japanese literature. Both beauty and sadness are resolved in the last group of poems, those on mixed topics (*zō*), where all that has gone before is recapitulated. In nine poems the adult life of a courtier with a religious bent passes before us: his early success, a hint of love, his failure to advance in the world, his effort to retreat from it, his inevitable return to the world for a last glimpse, and his final attainment of the Buddhist awareness that in this world the sorrows of human existence are inescapable. This pattern not only harmonizes sadness and beauty but amounts to a philosophy of life.[32] From the conventional opening of the *Kindai Shūka* with a spring poem to the increasingly sad overtones of the last poems, there is a coherent development that makes an esthetic whole out of eighty-three poems selected from poetry written over a period of five centuries.

One other technique contributed to the integration of the *Kindai Shūka*: there is a chronological element in the ordering of the poems. Although this principle, which dominates Western anthologies, is rare in Japanese Court poetry, it does occasionally appear. The first two books of the *Man'yōshū* are ordered chronologically, as are numerous subgroups of poems in the imperial anthologies. Teika himself used the principle in the *Hyakunin Shūka* and the *Hyakunin Isshu*. There is no rigid adherence to chronology in the *Kindai Shūka*, but there is sporadic attention to it. Each of the major sections of the sequence ends with a poem by a *Shinkokin* poet—a poet of Shunzei's or Teika's generation represented in the *Shinkokinshū*. The seasonal poems are thus ended by Yoshitsune, the laments by Sai-

---

[32] The final group of poems on mixed topics gives the *Kindai Shūka* the structural balance and richness of tone that is missing from Teika's 103-poem sequence in the *Eiga Taigai*, which ends, rather abruptly, with a section on love, but which is otherwise similar to the *Kindai Shūka* in structure and content, viz.: spring, 16 poems; summer, 6; autumn, 31; winter, 11; congratulatory, 1; laments, 6; parting, 2; travel, 5; love, 25.

gyō, the travel poems by Ietaka, the love poems by Saigyō, and the poems on mixed topics, as well as the total sequence, by Shunzei. With this device, Teika indicates his high valuation of these modern poems, lends them additional prominence and prestige, and emphasizes the poets he most admires.

It is, however, the principles of association and progression that do most to integrate the sequence and make it pleasurable reading. The subsequences often function independently of the main plot. This is especially true of the spatial progressions in the love sequence. The main plot, the progression of a courtly love affair, is enacted either in the capital or close by. But the subsequence chases merrily up and down the coastlines and hinterlands of Japan, at one point even going to China and back. This playing off of a fixed situation, advancing toward an inexorable end, against a seemingly irrational counterpoint of rapid movement is especially attractive and especially Japanese.

Constructing such a pattern requires a good deal of manipulation by the compiler. Teika sometimes alters the original conception of a poem by placing it in a position within the sequence that alters its topic.[33] Poem 37 appears among the poems on mixed topics in the *Kokinshū,* but Teika finds it convenient to treat it as the first of the travel poems, since it has elements both of travel and of parting, the preceding category. Poem 55 is a summer poem in the *Gosenshū,* a love poem in Teika's se-

---

[33] In his *Nishidaishū* Teika changed the categories of some eighty poems from what they had been in their original anthologies and placed poems earlier or later in a given category than they originally had been. These changes reflect his concern with association and progression. As Higuchi Yoshimaro points out in an analysis of a subsequence of nine spring poems in the *Nishidaishū,* "The poems are linked together by Teika's own individual consciousness of compilation and order." (*Teika Hachidaishō to Kenkyū,* II, 96.) Since the poems of the *Kindai Shūka* appear in the same order in the *Kindai Shūka* and the *Nishidaishū,* one may assume that the alterations in the traditional categories of certain poems were made for the *Nishidaishū* and not specifically for the *Kindai Shūka.* But in the later work, of course, Teika raised new associations by juxtaposing the poems in a new way.

33

quence. Teika may have decided independently to alter its category, or he may have had in mind its treatment as a love poem in the *Yamato Monogatari,* a mid-tenth-century collection of "tales of poems."[34] Certainly the poem looks like a love allegory. In any event, Teika consciously changed the speaker from a woman to a man. Such manipulations, and perhaps integration itself, are made possible by certain features of Japanese poetry: the rarity with which the sex of the speaker is made explicit, the fact that personal pronouns are seldom used, and the lack of distinctions of person or number in the nouns and verbs of the language. Without this potential for variable interpretation Teika could scarcely manipulate the poems as he does.

Of course the manipulation is not capricious. The concluding group of poems, for example, is treated as if it has a single speaker. This device shows most clearly how the new juxtaposition of poems endows certain elements in them with a different, and often more important, function than they originally had. Poem 78, for example, contains the word *chigiri,* which in the context established by the poem's headnote in the *Senzaishū* means "promise" of a favor from a high lord. The omission of all headnotes allows Teika to stress the traditional love associations of the word. The promise therefore becomes a lover's promise, as well as a promise of worldly favors, and thus provides a smooth transition from the speaker's life of gallantry in the preceding poem to consideration of his worldly career in the following one. The alteration of topics and meanings is one of the most important operative principles in the integration of poetic sequences. Nature imagery was especially suitable for this treatment, since it was often used allegorically for love. Compilers of sequences could, therefore, draw suggestions of love from poems originally composed on nature, or, conversely, stress the natural elements in a series of love poems.

[34] "Tales of poems" (*utamonogatari*) are short episodes that provide a prose context for occasional poems.

The love poems make up the longest unit in the *Kindai Shūka,* and in integrating them Teika achieves some of his most striking effects. The most important technique he employs to re-create the experience of love is a shifting point of view. Within the love sequence there are three groups of poems. The first group focuses on the lover, and is presented from his point of view. In the second, the point of view shifts back and forth as the courtship grows more intense and the lady begins to respond. The last group is presented from the point of view of the lady, who has been betrayed by her lover. This shifting point of view both reflects and underscores the irony at the heart of the love affair. During the early stages of the courtship, the man is distraught with love, and the woman coolly rejects him. But almost as soon as the affair is begun the man betrays her, and the woman who had been so cold is left passionately involved, almost to the point of mental and physical collapse. The beautiful and tragic unfolding of her betrayal is the height of the story's interest.

The details of this narrative pattern illustrate Teika's artistry. The love sequence consists of poems 41 to 74. In the first eight poems, the courtier becomes interested in the lady and tries to interest her in him. The next two alternate the lady's point of view (49) and the courtier's (50). At this point there is one poem (51) of general comment on the nature of love, which introduces a wider point of view. This poem, which is both interesting in itself and crucial to the sequence, prefigures the inevitable end of the courtly affair even before the lovers have been joined. More than this, it corresponds to poems of general statement at other important points in the sequence, such as the first of the laments (30) and the last poem on mixed topics (83). In the next twelve poems (52–63), the point of view alternates dramatically; the lady declares her love in poem 56, just before the middle of the love sequence. The group ends with eleven poems from the lady's point of view, in which all the patterns of association and progression except the temporal progression of the affair are dissolved one by one. With poem 71 the spatial progression is suspended until the poems on mixed topics begin, and with poem 72 the association of images becomes quite tenuous. The steady reduction of integrating techniques and the concentration on the forsaken woman's unfolding emotions, from indignation to bitterness, from bitterness to despair, from despair to renewed indignation, and finally to anguished reminiscence, produce a muted beauty recalling some of the finest passages in *The Tale of Genji*. Through the entire *Kindai Shūka* Teika moves smoothly from one category to another, and the simple beginning of the sequence is subtly transformed into a complex, life-encompassing experience.

A few comments on our procedures and principles of translation may help the reader on his way. The role of a poem in the sequence has at times determined how we have rendered the sex of the poem's speaker, and whether nouns, pronouns, and verbs are given in the singular or plural. To discover the meaning of a particular poem, we have often referred to the headnote accompanying the poem in the anthology from which Teika selected it, or considered its placement in his *Nishidaishū*. We have tried, however, not to disrupt the spirit of his sequence by obtruding such information. At the same time, we have often felt it necessary to expand upon the bare statement of the original. No method of translation is immune to criticism, but in no language is poetry a matter of bare statement, and it could hardly be one in translations from a language and culture now so distant from ours. The expanded imagery and added detail of the translations, which are intended to draw out nuances of phrasing and implications of images and situations, are based on the learned commentaries of Japanese scholars, or on numerous poems on the same subjects in the first eight imperial anthologies and the many private collections that supplement them.

Introduction

Our translation of *Superior Poems of Our Time* is the first complete translation into any language of an integrated Japanese poetic sequence, although in *Japanese Court Poetry* we translated two short subsequences (pp. 319–29, 403–13) and analyzed the techniques of association and progression that integrated them. Our intent in this translation is to supply the information necessary to an understanding of the poems both as separate entities and as units in a larger sequence. The transliterated poems are followed by two kinds of commentary. The first places the poem in the imperial anthology in which it was first "published," identifies the poet, and quotes the headnote with its statement of topic, or absence of specific topic, and situation. (We have also indicated the other anthologies attributed to Teika in which the poems appear.) The second indicates the use of such techniques as pillow-words or pivot-words (see Glossary, pp. 141–42), cites significant textual variants, comments on striking or difficult matters of translation, and provides translations of earlier poems alluded to. These notes are intended to elucidate the individual poems. The notes accompanying the translations, under the rubrics Time, Space, and Motifs, explicate the development of the sequence, tracing the temporal and spatial progressions and the associational techniques that integrate the poems. Inevitably, these rubrics sometimes overlap and oversimplify, but even a much more detailed and rigidly applied scheme of analysis could hardly convey all the delicate nuances of the original Japanese. At the same time, we have repeatedly specified the occurrence or continuance of images and situations that the reader will find obvious, in the hope that such information will prove more helpful than gratuitous in making the pattern of association and progression clear at every point in the sequence.

Superior Poems of Our Time

PREFATORY ESSAY

> This is now a thing of the distant past. Having been asked by a certain person how poetry ought to be composed, I wrote down just as they occurred to my foolish mind the few things of which I had gained some understanding. I put this together in common language completely lacking in style and sent it off. It looks very poor, but it represents my own personal views, mistaken though they may be.[1]

The art of Japanese poetry appears to be shallow but is deep, appears to be easy but is difficult. And the number of people who understand and know about it is not large. Tsurayuki, in ancient times, preferred a style in which the conception of the poem was clever, the loftiness of tone difficult to achieve, the diction strong, and the effect pleasing and tasteful, but he did not compose in the style of overtones and ethereal beauty.[2] Ever since, those who have received his heritage have for the most part inclined toward his style. However, as the times have degenerated, so have people's minds; later poets have not been able to attain Tsurayuki's level, and their diction has grown ever more vulgar. This is particularly the case with men of the recent past, who have given the first importance simply to stringing together thirty syllables on any idea that happened to

---

[1] The preamble was amended for the holograph by the addition of an opening sentence and some changes in wording. Teika added "just as they occurred" (*makasete*), "sent it off" (*okurihaberishi*), and "mistaken though they may be" (*higagoto*), and substituted "had gained some understanding" (*omoietaru*) for "having some ability to judge" (*omoiwakimauru*). Although the changes are slight, they make it clear that Teika has returned to the essay after a considerable lapse of time. See the text of the version sent away in *NKGT*, III, 326. Teika's reference to Sanetomo as "a certain person" is perhaps best explained by the desire not to appear boastful by naming his high connections.

[2] For a discussion of the poetry of Tsurayuki and his age, see *JCP*, Chap. V.

come into their heads, and who have had no conception whatever of poetic style or standards of diction.[3] Because of this, the poetry of these last degenerate days has been like the country bumpkin leaving the shelter of the blossoms or the merchant taking off his gorgeous robes. Nevertheless, the Major Counselor Lord Tsunenobu, Shunrai Ason, the Mayor of the Left Division of the Capital (Lord Akisuke), Kiyosuke Ason, and, more recently, his Lordship my late father, or rather the person known as Mototoshi, under whom he studied this art—these men departed from the vulgar poetic styles of a degenerate age and sought to recapture the styles of the poetry of old.[4] The finest poems by these men, composed with careful thought, are perhaps equal to those of high antiquity. And in the present generation have appeared a number of poems in which the poets have sought to improve the vulgar styles to some slight degree and have shown a preference for the old diction, so that a time has come when something of the proper style of poetry, which had been lost since the time of the Bishop of Kazan, the Middle Commander Ariwara, Sosei, and Komachi, has been seen and heard again—although certain people who have no understanding of the nature of things no doubt say that something altogether new has appeared and that the art of poetry has changed.[5]

[3] The tanka of course has thirty-one syllables, but in writing of poetry the medieval critics often used the round number thirty.

[4] Minamoto Tsunenobu was noted for his new poetry of natural description in the "lofty style" (*taketakaki tei*), and was a leading innovator of his generation. His position was inherited by his son Shunrai, a more radical and idiosyncratic poet, who led the innovating forces against Fujiwara Mototoshi, Shunzei's first teacher. Fujiwara Akisuke and his son Kiyosuke were leaders of the Rokujō family, competitors of the house of Shunzei and Teika. The conservative Rokujō poets were more noted for their scholarship than their poetry, but many of them were accomplished poets and they were receptive to the styles of descriptive poetry being developed in their day. Teika obviously admired Akisuke and Kiyosuke, if not other Rokujō poets. Teika politely attributes the achievement of his father to Mototoshi, but Shunzei admired Mototoshi more for his learning than his art.

[5] The "Bishop of Kazan" is Bishop Henjō; "Middle Commander Ariwara" is Ariwara Narihira. Together with the poetess Ono no Komachi, they are the best known of the Six Poetic Geniuses.

The students of the art among the younger generation today appear sincerely to think that they are composing real poetry, while actually they know nothing about its proper style. They make a fetish of obscurity, changing what ought to be simple into something difficult, yoking together things that have no relation to one another—perhaps because it has become universal for people to choose the most inappropriate poems as models.[6] For my part, I fully realize that I ought to have a thorough knowledge of poetry, whereas I have merely inherited the fame of two generations.[7] At times I have been treated with honor, at times been spoken of with scorn, but lacking sufficient devotion to this art from the very beginning, I have learned nothing except how to put together a few odds and ends that people have refused to accept as poetry. Although my father's only instructions to me were the simple words, "Poetry is not an art which can be learned by looking afield or hearing afar; it is something that proceeds from the heart and is understood in the self," I never even groped my way far enough to experience the truth of what he said. How much the less can I do so now, having crossed the threshold of old age, and sunk to my present wretched condition with many illnesses and deep suffering. I have forgotten the color of the flowers of words; the wellsprings of inspiration have run dry. I have not even been composing any poetry at all, so that more and more I have tended to give up thinking about it, and have forgotten what little I once knew. All I shall do is make one or two trifling remarks, and those only about the poetic styles that I at present prefer.

[6] At the end of the version sent away, Teika explains further: "What I mean by changing what ought to be simple into something difficult and yoking together things that have no relation to one another are such expressions as 'the wind falls' and 'the snow blows,' or 'the floating wind' and 'the first clouds.' " (*NKGT,* III, 330; Hisamatsu and Nishio, p. 111.) The normal expressions would be "the wind blows" and "the snow falls," "the floating clouds" and "the first wind."

[7] In copying the Prefatory Essay from the version sent away, Teika omitted a clause here, probably on purpose, viz., "I fully realize that *a person such as myself who has no knowledge or discrimination in this art,* ought to...." The omission does not affect the general sense of the passage.

If in diction you admire the traditional, if in treatment you attempt the new, if you aim at an unobtainably lofty effect, and if you study the poetry of Kampei and before—then how can you fail to succeed?[8] With regard to preferring the old, the practice of taking the words of an ancient poem and incorporating them into one's own composition without changing them is known as "using a foundation poem."[9] However, I feel that if one uses, say, the second and third lines of such a foundation poem, just as they are, in the first three lines of one's own poem, and then goes on to use the last two lines of it in the same fashion, it will prove impossible to make something that sounds like a new poem. Depending on the style, it may be best to avoid using the first two lines of the foundation poem.[10] For example, without using over and over such conventional expressions as "The capital, / Ancient as Furu in Iso no Kami," "The fifth month, / When the wood thrush sings," "The Heavenly Hill of Kagu, / Lovely as the distant sky," "The traveler on the road / Straight as a courtier's spear," it would be impossible to compose any poetry at all.[11] But I was taught that one must not use

[8] Strictly speaking, the Kampei era was from 889 to 897, but Teika is using the term "Kampei and before" to designate the Age of the Six Poetic Geniuses. A more explicit version of this sentence opens the Prefatory Essay of the *Eiga Taigai*. "In diction do not depart from the anthologies of the three eras [i.e., the first three imperial anthologies]. Seek for a conception no one has ever used and use that in your poem." *Eiga Taigai*, in *NKGT*, III, 339; Hisamatsu and Nishio, p. 114.

[9] The term *honka* is still used today. Teika is of course talking about the technique of allusive variation, usually termed *honkadori*, literally "taking a foundation poem."

[10] The corresponding passage in the *Eiga Taigai* is as follows: "In composing a new poem by taking an old one, using as many as three lines out of the five is using far too many, for there would be no effect of novelty. However, it is permissible to use two lines and three or four syllables of a third. Furthermore, it is extremely undesirable to use the words of the old poem to express the same thing in the new, such as using a poem on cherry blossoms for a poem on cherry blossoms, or a poem on the moon for one on the moon. But if you use a seasonal poem for a poem on love or on a mixed topic, or use a love poem or one on a mixed topic for a seasonal poem, then there is no harm in using an old poem." *NKGT*, III, 339; Hisamatsu and Nishio, p. 114.

[11] These expressions are in Japanese: *Iso no Kami / Furuki miyako; Hototogisu / Naku ya satsuki; Hisakata no / Ama no Kaguyama;* and *Tamaboko*

44

such famous lines as "The Old Year not yet gone, / The longed-for spring has come at last," "The stream / That wet my sleeves in summer as I drank," "What now is real? / This moon, this spring are altered," "This wind that scatters cherry flowers / Beneath the trees," and the like.[12] Next, with regard to poems by one's fellow poets, even if they are no longer living, if they have been composed so recently that they might be said to have been written yesterday or today, I think it essential to avoid using any part of such a poem, even a single line, that is distinc-

---

no / Michiyukibito. All except the second consist of a 5-syllable pillow-word, or conventional epithet, with a following noun or phrase of 6 or 7 syllables that it commonly modified. The second example is a "preface" used with a final noun. Such expressions from the traditional "word hoard" were often used for the first two lines of a tanka, and Teika is saying that if this were not allowed it would be impossible to write poetry.

[12] These famous lines are the first two lines from poems by Motokata, Narihira, and Tsurayuki. Those by Motokata (*Toshi no uchi ni / Haru wa kinikeri;* see p. 26 above) are taken from the opening poem of the *Kokinshū.* Those by Narihira are from his most famous poem (in the *Kokinshū,* XV:747).

Tsuki ya aranu	What now is real?
Haru ya mukashi no	This moon, this spring, are altered
Haru naranu	From their former being—
Waga mi hitotsu wa	While this alone, my mortal body, remains
Moto no mi ni shite.	As ever changed by love beyond all change.

The lines by Tsurayuki are from two of his most celebrated poems (from the *Kokinshū,* I:2, and the *Shūishū,* I:64).

Sode hijite	Will the breeze
Musubishi mizu no	That blows on this first day of spring
Kōreru o	Dissolve the winter ice,
Haru tatsu kyō no	Releasing the pent-up memory of the stream
Kaze ya toku ran.	That wet my sleeves in summer as I drank?

Sakura chiru	It is not cold,
Ko no shitakaze wa	This wind that scatters cherry flowers
Samukarade	Beneath the trees:
Sora ni shirarenu	It blows a whirl of white snow petals
Yuki zo furikeru.	In a storm the sky has never known.

Teika's point is that only the first two lines of such famous poems as these should be avoided as a basis for allusive variation—not necessarily the rest of the poem or the poem as a whole. He would have allowed such a poem to be used for allusive variation provided the poet alluded to less famous lines or echoed the poem in a more subtle way. Of course the more famous the poem, the more subtle the allusion could be.

45

tive enough to be recognized as the work of a particular poet.[13]

These things merely represent the few ideas I have, for I have never studied or learned anything about general principles of evaluating poetry, of telling the bad from the good.[14] Still less

[13] Again the *Eiga Taigai* is more specific: "Under no circumstances is it permissible to use expressions which were first employed in poems of the last seventy or eighty years." (*NKGT*, III, 339; Hisamatsu and Nishio, p. 114.) In both the *Eiga Taigai* and the *Kindai Shūka*, as well as in the *Maigetsushō*, Teika adumbrates the concept of *nushi aru kotoba*, "expressions that have owners." The concept was further elaborated by Tameie, who drew up a list of forty-eight such expressions. Many quarrels over which expressions should be added to the list divided Tameie's descendants. See Tameie's *Yakumo Kuden*, in *NKGT*, III, 398–99.

Teika's concern with allusive variation reflects the fact that he did more than any other poet of his day to spread the technique and demonstrate its rich potential to the younger poets of the age of the *Shinkokinshū*. His most detailed and explicit statement on allusive variation is in the *Maigetsushō*: "In regard to the method of taking a foundation poem ... it is only for the most accomplished poets to use a poem on cherry blossoms just as it is for one of their own on cherry blossoms, or a poem on the moon for one on the moon. Ordinarily, there should be some change—with a poem on spring used for one on autumn or winter, or a poem on love incorporated into one on a mixed or seasonal topic—yet done in such a way that it is clear that one has used the older poem. Taking too many of the words of the foundation poem must be avoided. The proper method is perhaps to use two phrases or so that seem to be the very essence of the poem and space them out between the upper and lower verses of the new one.

"Take the following poem [*Kokinshū*, XI:484], for example:

Yūgure wa	Since the one I love
Kumo no hatate ni	Is a person inhabiting a realm
Mono zo omou	Lofty in the heavens,
Amatsusora naru	I turn my longing in the evening
Hito o kou tote.	Toward the tips of the purple-tinted clouds.

Here, one might take the words 'tips of the purple-tinted clouds' [*kumo no hatate*] and 'I turn my longing' [*mono omou*]; place them in the upper and lower verses; and make the new poem on a mixed or seasonal topic or something other than love.... I have been told that it is bad to use too many phrases that are so unusual and striking that they are the chief distinction of the foundation poem. On the other hand, since it is also said that nothing is accomplished by employing a poem in such an obscure way that it does not look as if one had used it at all, one must be sure to understand such matters when taking a foundation poem." *Maigetsushō*, in *NKGT*, III, 350; Hisamatsu and Nishio, pp. 132–33.

[14] Teika accepted Shunzei's view that the good and the bad in poetry were rather to be felt than expressed. Shunzei had written that one poetic handbook or treatise was much like another, and such works were of little help. *Korai Fūteishō*, in *NKGT*, II, 303–4.

do I know about the explication of difficult passages and things of that sort, concerning which I understand that each poetic house and family has its own special customs and traditions, for I never had anything about such matters passed on to me by my father. Then, too, since the little knowledge I have differs in no respect from what various other people have recorded, it would be superfluous for me to write it down all over again myself, although the views of other poetic houses apparently differ somewhat from my own.[15]

---

[15] Although there was general agreement on fundamentals, each school had its own traditions of scholarship and poetic practice. The Rokujō family emphasized scholarship, exegesis, and poetic lore more than practice, as the handbooks and treatises compiled by Kiyosuke and Kenshō attest. The Mikohidari, by contrast, emphasized the overriding importance of the creative act: concentration, self-discipline, practice, and the intuitive grasp of the poetic essence of a subject. In protesting his ignorance to Sanetomo, who had asked for instructions on "the Six Principles and the Poetic Styles," Teika is of course being modest, and perhaps evasive—unready to reveal to a novice all the secrets of his art. At the same time, he is suggesting that a knowledge of such matters is neither the special concern of his house nor particularly conducive to the writing of good poetry. Cf. Kazamaki Keijirō, "Fujiwara Teika ni yotte haaku sareta mono," *Nihon Bungakushi no Kenkyū*, I, 346–68.

The following abbreviations for the Man'yōshū and the imperial anthologies antedating the Kindai Shūka are used in the notes to the sequence that begins on the next page: MYS Man'yōshū (749); KKS Kokinshū (905); GSS Gosenshū (951); SIS Shūishū (1000); GSIS Goshūishū (1086); KYS Kin'yōshū (1125); SKS Shikashū (1153); SZS Senzaishū (1188); SKKS Shinkokinshū (1206).

The following abbreviations designate works by Teika or works attributed to him: TKJT Teika Jittei; KSB Kensōbon, or "version sent away"; NSDS Nishidaishū; EGTG Eiga Taigai; SKDT Shūka no Daitai; HNSK Hyakunin Shūka; HDSSI Hachidaishū Shūitsu; HNIS Hyakunin Isshu. These works are briefly described in the Bibliography, pp. 145–46.

1]   Haru tatsu to
            Iu bakari ni ya
            Mi-Yoshino no
            Yama mo kasumite
            Kesa wa miyu ran.

Mibu no Tadamine (fl. ca. 910), SIS, I: 1. "Composed for a poetry contest at the house of Taira Sadabumi."

Yama mo expresses surprise that haze, the sign of early spring, has come "even to the mountains" of Yoshino on the first day of the season. (It was normally thought that spring came late to such mountain fastnesses.) A fanciful reason is suggested: perhaps the haze "knows" this is the first day of spring in the Court calendar, and that is why it has come. *Mi-* (fair) is a decorative prefix used with certain place names.

NSDS 2, EGTG 1, SKDT 3, HDSSI 21

2]   Yamazakura
            Sakisomeshi yori
            Hisakata no
            Kumoi ni miyuru
            Taki no shiraito.

Minamoto Shunrai (1055–1129). KYS, I: 50. "Composed on cherry blossoms at the house of the Uji Former Prime Minister."

Hisakata no: pillow-word for *kumoi* (clouds), *hikari* (light), and other celestial phenomena; of uncertain meaning, its amplifying force is clearly that of a loftiness and brightness of tone.

KSB 4, NSDS 95, EGTG 7, HNSK 76, HDSSI 41

48

SEASONAL POEMS

Spring

1]   Is it just because
They say this is the day which marks
  The coming of the spring
That even the mountains of fair Yoshino
Are veiled this morning in a haze?

Time Progression: first day of spring
Space Progression: mountains viewed from afar
Motifs: haze

2]   Since first they flowered,
The mountain cherries have seemed to be
  The white cascades
Of a celestial waterfall that streams
From the distant cloudland of the sky.

Time: from beginning of spring to cherry-blossom season
Space: mountains viewed somewhat more closely
Motifs: celestial imagery continued—haze of poem 1 is now clouds; cherry
 blossoms

3]   Sakura saku
          Tōyamadori no
          Shidario no
          Naganagashi hi mo
          Akanu iro kana.

Ex-Emperor Go-Toba (1180–1239). SKKS, II: 99. "Composed for a folding screen depicting cherry trees in bloom on the mountains, on the occasion of the celebration at the Bureau of Poetry of the ninetieth birthday of Shunzei."

The poem is an allusive variation on a poem attributed to Hitomaro (poem 64 in this sequence). The first three lines form a "preface" (*jo*) for the last two, with the juncture at *naganagashi* (long).

NSDS 99, EGTG 8, HDSSI 71

4]   Iza kyō wa
          Haru no yamabe ni
          Majirinan
          Kurenaba nage no
          Hana no kage ka wa.

Priest Sosei (fl. ca. 890). KKS, II: 95. "Composed on a visit to the Imperial Prince of the Urin'in when he went out into the northern mountains to view the cherry blossoms."

NSDS 115, EGTG 11

3]   Even through a day,
A day as long as the flowing tail
   Of the mountain fowl,
The cherries flowering white on distant hills
Possess a beauty that can never pall.

Time: cherry blossoms at their height
Space: hills or mountains at a distance
Motifs: cherry blossoms and hills, continued; *iro* (color, beauty) is associated
  with *shira-* (white) of 2

4]   Come, just for today
Let us lose ourselves in wandering
   Deep in spring hills—
If darkness falls, how can we fail to find
A place to sleep beneath those blossoming
     boughs?

Time: cherry blossoms continue at their height
Space: movement into the hills
Motifs: cherry blossoms and hills, continued

5]   Sakuragari
           Ame wa furikinu
           Onajiku wa
           Nuru to mo hana no
           Kage ni kakuren.

Anonymous. SIS, I: 50. "Topic unknown."
NSDS 116, EGTG 12

6]   Hana no iro wa
           Utsurinikeri na
           Itazura ni
           Waga mi yo ni furu
           Nagame seshi ma ni.

Ono no Komachi (fl. ca. 850). KKS, II: 113. "Topic unknown."
Iro: color, form, or appearance, with overtones of passion. *Furu* pivots
"grow old" and "fall"; *nagame* pivots "ponder vacantly" (especially about
love) and "long rain."
TKJT 45, NSDS 122, EGTG 13, HNSK 13, HDSSI 1, HNIS 9

52

5]   Hunting for blossoms,
     I have been caught in a sudden shower—
        Well then, let it pour:
     Though I am drenched I shall be sheltered
     Beneath these flowering cherry boughs.

Time: onset of rains, which augurs the fall of the blossoms
Space: still in hills, speaker has gone under the trees seen in 4
Motifs: cherry blossoms and hills, continued; rain; the suggestion of shelter
     in 4 is realized here with cherry trees sheltering speaker; identical diction
     with 4 (*hana no kage*)

6]   The color of these flowers
     No longer has allure, and I am left
        To ponder unavailingly
     The desire that my beauty once aroused
     Before it fell in this long rain of time.

Time: blossoms are fading
Space: spatial progression suspended until autumn poems begin
Motifs: cherry blossoms and rain, continued; contrast of mood with 5; hu-
     man concerns introduced

7]   Hisakata no
        Hikari nodokeki
        Haru no hi ni
        Shizugokoro naku
        Hana no chiru ran.

Ki no Tomonori (d. 905?). KKS, II: 84. "Composed on the falling of the cherry blossoms."
Hisakata no: pillow-word for *hikari* (radiance) suggesting loftiness and brightness of tone.

NSDS 150, EGTG 15, SKDT 24, HNSK 26, HNIS 33

8]   Natsu no yo wa
        Mada yoi nagara
        Akenuru o
        Kumo no izuko ni
        Tsuki nokoru ran.

Kiyowara Fukayabu (fl. ca. 905–30). KKS, III: 166. "Composed toward dawn on a night of a beautiful moon."
Nokoru in KKS and in Shunzei's *Korai Fūteishō* reads *yadoru*: "spend the night," "take shelter." The speaker has stayed up through the night, so absorbed by the beauty of the moon and the dawn that the night seems to have all passed by in a moment.

NSDS 252, HNSK 33, HNIS 36

7]   On this day in spring
           When the radiance of the air
              Breathes tranquility,
           Why should the cherry petals flutter
           With unsettled heart to earth?

Time: end of spring
Motifs: human concerns, continued; celestial and light imagery reintro-
   duced; cherry blossoms personified; this poem harmonizes the contrasting
   moods of 5 and 6

           Summer

8]   On a summer night
           So short that daybreak fills the sky
              In early evening,
           Where does the moon, its long journey scarce
                 begun,
           Find temporary shelter in the clouds?

Time: summer, night, have come, but they both end as soon as they begin—
   with this poem
Motifs: personification of natural phenomena, celestial imagery, continued;
   phrasing of last line similar to that of 7

9]   Yaemugura
Shigereru yado no
Sabishiki ni
Hito koso miene
Aki wa kinikeri.

Priest Egyō (fl. ca. 985). SIS, III: 140. "When people were composing poems at the Kawara Palace on the topic, 'Autumn Comes to a Dilapidated Dwelling.'"

NSDS 274, EGTG 24, HNSK 52, HDSSI 22, HNIS 47

10]   Aware ika ni
Kusaba no tsuyu no
Koboru ran
Akikaze tachinu
Miyagino no hara.

Priest Saigyō (1118–90). SKKS, IV: 300. "Topic unknown."
Kusaba (leaves of plants): although the general word is used, Miyagino was famous for its bush clover, the image probably intended; the more general term may suggest consideration from afar. *Ran* (must be dripping): the presumptive form again suggests that the speaker is far from Miyagino. Saigyō is said to have composed the poem on his return from a journey there, although it appears in his personal poetry contest, *Mimosusogawa Utaawase*. *Hara* suggests the wide space of the plain.

TKJT 127, NSDS 286, EGTG 26, HDSSI 72

Autumn

9]   In the loneliness
Of my wretched dwelling overgrown
    With wild grasses,
Although no human visitor appears,
The melancholy autumn has come.

Time: autumn begins, by convention, overnight; daytime implied, follow-
   ing passage of night in 8
Space: progression resumed, with the speaker in an isolated place
Motifs: personification of nature, continued; plants-grass imagery

10]   How thickly the dew
Must be dripping from the leaves of plants:
    The autumn wind
Has risen over the wide clover fields
On the land's-end plain of Miyagi.

Time: early autumn, daytime, continued
Space: isolated and remote region, continued, although the speaker imag-
   ines the place described from a distance
Motifs: plants-grass imagery, continued; dew suggests the tears of loneliness
   implicit in the situations of 9 and 11

57

11]   Tsuki mireba
            Chiji ni mono koso
            Kanashikere
            Waga mi hitotsu no
            Aki ni wa aranedo.

Ōe no Chisato (fl. ca. 890–905). KKS, IV: 193. "Composed at a poetry contest at the residence of Prince Koresada."
The poem is founded upon a contrast between *chiji* (a thousand things) and *hitotsu* (one's self).

TKJT 225, NSDS 306, EGTG 27, HNSK 30, HNIS 23

12]   Aki no tsuyu ya
            Tamoto ni itaku
            Musubu ran
            Nagaki yo akazu
            Yadoru tsuki kana.

Go-Toba. SKKS, IV: 433. "Among some autumn poems."
The personification of the moon contrasts with the image of dew, which is used metaphorically for tears. *Musubu* (gathers, congeals) conveys the passage of time.

NSDS 312, EGTG 31, HDSSI 73

11]   A thousand things
        Overcome me with their sadness
          As I gaze upon the moon,
        Although autumn surely was not meant
        To be felt by my one self alone.

Time: autumn advancing; night
Space: isolated location, continued
Motifs: sadness, continued; moon image introduced

12]   Is this that gathers
        Ever more heavily on my sleeves
          The autumn dew,
        Giving through the long night a lodging
        To the unwearying brilliance of the moon?

Time: autumn, night, continued
Space: isolation, continued; indoors location of speaker implicit in situation
Motifs: dew-tears relationship of preceding poems is explicitly realized; sadness, continued; moon is personified as faithful friend or lover giving companionship to speaker

13]　　　Aki no tsuki
　　　Takane no kumo no
　　　　Anata nite
　　　Hareyuku sora no
　　　Kururu machikeri.

Fujiwara Tadamichi (1097–1164). szs, IV: 274. "Composed for a sequence of thirty poems on the moon."

NSDS 314

14]　　　Nakiwataru
　　　Kari no namida ya
　　　　Ochitsu ran
　　　Mono omou yado no
　　　Hagi no ue no tsuyu.

Anonymous. KKS, IV: 221. "Topic unknown."
This famous poem has strong overtones of love: *mono omou yado* (my grieving house) suggests that the speaker is a woman who has sat up through the night grieving over her lover's neglect.

TKJT 8, NSDS 324, EGTG 32, HDSSI 2

13]   Somewhere beyond
       The clouds that lie upon the peaks,
          The autumn moon
       Delayed its coming till the sky
       Was fully cleared and darkness fell.

Time: autumn, night, continued
Space: progression to another dwelling beyond mountains is implied
Motifs: personification of moon, continued—like a human lover, the moon
   waits for nightfall to visit speaker

14]   Are these the tears
       Shed by the geese whose cries of passage
          Rent the painful night—
       The morning dew upon bush-clover flowers
       In the garden of my grieving house?

Time: autumn; morning following night of 13
Space: speaker is in the dwelling implied in 13, looking outside
Motifs: resumption of dew-tears trope for human emotions; reason for tears
   is love, by association of *mono omou yado* with waiting of 13; human
   lover suggested in 12 and 13 has failed to come; geese associate with sky
   of 13

15]   Aki no ta no
           Kario no io no
              Toma o arami
           Waga koromode wa
           Tsuyu ni nuretsutsu.

Attributed to Emperor Tenchi (614–71). GSS, VI: 302. "Topic unknown."
   Toma: a temporary field hut built to shelter the watchman who guards the grain from predators. The speaker is in the dilapidated hut, his sleeves wet with dew-tears. It has also been suggested that the Emperor, seeing the ruined hut, is shedding tears of compassion for the people's sufferings.
   TKJT 12, NSDS 332, EGTG 34, SKDT 54, HNSK 1, HDSSI 13, HNIS 1

16]   Shiratsuyu ni
           Kaze no fukishiku
              Aki no no wa
           Tsuranukitomenu
           Tama zo chirikeru.

Bunya Asayasu (fl. ca. 910). GSS, VI: 308. "Composed at imperial command in the Engi era."
   NSDS 360, EGTG 35, HNSK 38, HDSSI 12, HNIS 37

15]   With its thatch in ruin,
      The roof of the watch hut in the fields
        Admits the autumn,
     And it is this that day by day
     Brings yet more dew to wet my sleeves.

Time: autumn, morning, continued
Space: lonely dwelling, continued; movement from house with garden of 14
   to hut in paddy fields
Motifs: dew-tears trope, continued; destructive effects of elements intro-
   duced

16]   On the autumn moors
      The wind blows aslant the grasses
        Laden with white dew,
     Scattering upon the ground
     The broken strings of crystal beads.

Time: autumn, morning, continued
Space: from paddy fields to open moors
Motifs: dew, destructive effects of nature, continued; wind

17]   Akikaze ni
            Sasowarewataru
              Karigane wa
            Mono omou hito no
            Yado o yokanan.

Anonymous. GSS, VII: 360. "Topic unknown."
NSDS 378, EGTG 38, HDSSI 14

18]   Yū sareba
            Kadota no inaba
              Otozurete
            Ashi no maroya ni
            Akikaze zo fuku.

Minamoto Tsunenobu (1016–97). KYS, III: 183. "Composed on the topic,
'The Autumn Wind at a House in the Country,' when people went to visit
Lord Morokane's mountain villa at Umezu."
   Kadota: "gate fields," i.e., fields just beyond the enclosure about the
house. This poem is famous as an innovating poem in the style of descrip-
tive symbolism.
   TKJT 152, KSB 1, NSDS 402, EGTG 41, HNSK 70, HDSSI 43, HNIS 71

17]   Lured by the autumn wind,
        The geese wing by with mournful cries—
          Would that their path
        Were far distant from the dwelling
        Of one whose grief can bear no greater weight.

Time: autumn; daytime implied by position of poem in sequence
Space: return to the isolated dwelling
Motifs: wind, continued; dew image in 16 enforces the implication of tears
here by conventional dew-tears relationship and by association with *mono omou* (grief); sound imagery

18]   As evening falls,
        From across the fields of grain
          Beyond the fence,
        The autumn wind comes rustling
        In its visit to my reed-thatched hut.

Time: autumn; evening
Space: inside lonely dwelling, continued
Motifs: wind, sound imagery, continued (rustling of wind)

19]   Saoshika no
           Tsumadou yama no
           Okabe naru
           Wasada wa karaji
           Shimo wa oku to mo.

Attributed to Kakinomoto Hitomaro (fl. ca. 680–710). SKKS, V: 459. "Topic unknown."

Given as anonymous in MYS (X: 2220), where the headnote says "Composed on paddy fields," and the text for lines 2 and 5 varies: *Tsuma yobu yama no* and *Shimo wa furu to mo.*

TKJT 13, NSDS 418, EGTG 45, SKDT 73

20]   Okuyama ni
           Momiji fumiwake
           Naku shika no
           Koe kiku toki zo
           Aki wa kanashiki.

Sarumaru Dayū ? (fl. ca. 860?). KKS, IV: 215. "A poem from a poetry contest at the house of Prince Koresada."

Given as anonymous in KKS, but attributed to Sarumaru Dayū in *Hyakunin Isshu*; it also appears in *Sarumaru Dayū Shū*; originally composed for the *Kampei no Ontoki Kisai no Miya Utaawase.*

NSDS 422, EGTG 46, HNSK 8, HNIS 5

19]   Though soon the frost
        May fall upon the early ripened grain,
          I shall not reap
        Along those hillslopes where the stag
        Cries out so movingly for his mate.

Time: autumn advancing toward its close; night implied by stag's cries
Space: location of speaker unspecified, but probably in house near unseen
  fields
Motifs: fields, sound imagery, continued; mountain foothills, stag, intro-
  duced

20]   When I hear the stag
        Cry out deep within the mountains
          Where he picks his way
        Treading upon the fallen colored leaves,
        Then I feel the autumn truly sad.

Time: late autumn; night
Space: movement to mountain depths
Motifs: mountain, stag, sound imagery, continued; frost of 19 has its effect
  here in colored leaves

21]   Shiratsuyu mo
        Shigure mo itaku
        Moruyama wa
        Shitaba nokorazu
        Irozukinikeri.

Ki no Tsurayuki (868–945). KKS, V: 260. "Composed when in the vicinity of Moru mountain."
Moruyama pivots the place name and the verb *moru* (leak, fall).
NSDS 446, EGTG 49, HDSSI 3

22]   Honobono to
        Ariake no tsuki no
        Tsukikage ni
        Momiji fukiorosu
        Yamaoroshi no kaze.

Minamoto Saneakira (916–70). SKKS, VI: 591. "Topic unknown."
In *Saneakira Shū*, the personal collection of Saneakira, the poem has the headnote, "On a screen depicting people looking at fallen leaves." The repetitions (*tsuki no / Tsukikage* and *fukiorosu / Yamaoroshi*) are very unusual.
NSDS 486, EGTG 54

21]   On Moru mountain
Where the white dew and the drizzle
    Fall without ceasing,
Every last underleaf upon the trees
Has been dyed in some bright autumn hue.

Time: late autumn; dew implies dawn
Space: from mountain depths to more limited, closer mountain imagery
Motifs: leaves, mountains, continued

22]   Dimly, dimly,
In the pale radiance of the moon
    Lingering in the sky,
The mountain wind at dawn blows down
The few remaining autumn leaves.

Time: close of autumn; dawn, continued
Space: somewhat closer view than in 21
Motifs: mountain, leaf imagery, continued, with implied progression to the
    end of autumn as the last leaves fall

23]   Akishino ya
        Toyama no sato ya
        Shiguru ran
        Ikoma no take ni
        Kumo no kakareru.

Saigyō. SKKS, VI: 585. "Topic unknown."
The poem was originally composed for Saigyō's personal poetry contest,
the *Miyagawa Utaawase*, where the topic is "Winter Drizzle." Saigyō sent
the contest to Teika for judging, and this poem was scored the winner in
its round.

NSDS 504, EGTG 56, HDSSI 75

24]   Kimi kozu wa
        Hitori ya nenan
        Sasa no ha no
        Miyama mo soyo ni
        Sayagu shimoyo o.

Fujiwara Kiyosuke (1104–77). SKKS, VI: 616. "From a sequence of one hun-
dred poems humbly presented in the reign of ex-Emperor Sutoku."
An allusive variation on an envoy of a poem by Hitomaro on parting
from his wife (MYS, II: 133).

Sasa no ha wa	The bamboo grass
Miyama mo saya ni	Sighs in its tangled rustling
Midaru to mo	Deep within the mountains,
Ware wa imo omou	But my longing remains untangled
Wakarekinureba.	When I have left the one I love.

KSB 16, NSDS 514, EGTG 58

70

Winter

23]   Does the winter drizzle
Fall in Akishino on hamlets clustered
    In the outer mountains?
For upon the peak of Mount Ikoma
The clouds hang heavy with a storm.

Time: early winter; daytime
Space: to remoter mountains and back to nearer mountains
Motifs: the place name Akishino (literally, autumn bamboo grass) provides
    transition from autumn; clouds associate with wind in 22; mountain
    imagery, continued; hamlets suggest human society, anticipating love ele-
    ment of 24

24]   If you fail to come,
Must I lie alone and bear the sound
    Of the bamboo grass
Sighing deep within the mountains
As it rustles in the frosty night?

Time: winter; evening (waiting for lover)
Space: progression into the mountains, with suggestion that the speaker in-
    habits one of the hamlets mentioned in 23
Motifs: bamboo grass (sasa) associates with -shino of 23; mountains, contin-
    ued; frost (shimo-) begins subsequence of closely associated winter images

71

25]   Ama no hara
        Sora sae sae ya
        Wataru ran
        Kōri to miyuru
        Fuyu no yo no tsuki.

Priest Egyō ? sis, IV: 242. "Composed on gazing at the moon."
The poem is attributed to the priest Ambō in the *Konjaku Monogatari-shū*, and to Tsurayuki in the *Kokin Waka Rokujō*.

NSDS 545, HDSSI 23

26]   Furusato wa
        Yoshino no yama no
            Chikakereba
        Hitohi mo miyuki
        Furanu hi wa nashi.

Anonymous. kks, VI: 321. "Topic unknown."
kks text reads *yami shi* at end of second line, as do the *Nishidaishū* and *Eiga Taigai*. *Furusato* (ancient village, palace site): there had been in the Yoshino area an imperial villa from the reign of Ōjin (d. ca. 394) through that of Shōmu (d. 756).

NSDS 551, EGTG 61

25]   Do the heavenly plains
         And even the very sky so glisten
            For having frozen over,
         While shining as if it were pure ice,
         The moon lights up the winter night?

Time: midwinter; night
Space: indoors location, continued; speaker now contemplates a larger out-
   door panorama
Motifs: ice (*kōri*) is closely associated with frost (*shimo-*) of 24

26]   Once a palace site,
         But the mountains of Yoshino lie so close
            That this ancient village
         Is spared not even for a single day
         From the snow's relentless fall.

Time: midwinter; passage of a day
Space: speaker, now snowbound, is in the village implied in 24 (and by
   association in 25); subprogression of place names begins
Motifs: open view, continued; snow (*miyuki*) is closely associated with ice of
   25; reintroduction of place name

73

27]   Asaborake
Ariake no tsuki to
Miru made ni
Yoshino no sato ni
Fureru shirayuki.

Sakanoue Korenori (fl. ca. 910). KKS, VI: 332. "Composed on seeing the
fallen snow when he had gone down into the province of Yamato."
NSDS 558, EGTG 63, HNSK 29, HDSSI 4, HNIS 31

28]   Iso no kami
Furuno no ozasa
Shimo o hete
Hitoyo bakari ni
Nokoru toshi kana.

Fujiwara Yoshitsune (1169–1206). SKKS, VI: 698. "Topic unknown."
Iso no kami (place name): pillow-word for *Furu-*, which pivots the place
name Furu (in Yamato province) with "old." Lines 1–3 are a preface joined
to the statement of *hitoyo*, which pivots "single night" and "single joint."
NSDS 576, EGTG 64

74

27]   In the early dawn
It looks like the brightness of the moon
    Remaining in the sky,
The blanket of snow that through the night
Has covered the village of Yoshino.

Time: winter; dawn after passage of night
Space: the same village as in 26
Motifs: snow, place names, continued; reappearance of moon image of 25
   (implies that speaker has watched in vain throughout the night for visit
   from her beloved)

28]   Of the old year
Only a single short night remains,
    Short as the joints
Of bamboo grass withered by many frosts
Upon the moors of Furu in Iso no Kami.

Time: end of winter and of the seasonal poems; daytime
Space: movement from mountains to moors
Motifs: place names, continued; concern with time, explicit in 26 and im-
   plicit in 27, continued; withered bamboo grass marks end of speaker's
   winter of fruitless waiting, and echoes 24, where vigil was begun

29]   Kimi ga yo wa
        Tsukiji to zo omou
        Kamikaze ya
        Mimosusogawa no
        Suman kagiri wa.

Tsunenobu. GSIS, VII: 450. "Composed for a poetry contest at the Imperial Palace in 1078."
Kamikaze ya (the Land of the Divine Wind): pillow-word for Mimosuso-gawa. In the "version sent away," Teika writes that this poem and poems 75 and 76 below are "in the ideal style for poems on public occasions."
TKJT 153, KSB 2, NSDS 588, EGTG 65, HDSSI 34

30]   Sue no tsuyu
        Moto no shizuku ya
        Yo no naka no
        Okuresakidatsu
        Tameshi naru ran.

Bishop Henjō (816–90). SKKS, VIII: 757. "Topic unknown."
The *Henjō Shū* has the headnote, "On realizing the evanescence of life."
NSDS 635, EGTG 66

CONGRATULATORY POEM

29]   Our Sovereign's reign
Shall not end until the waters
 Of the Mimosuso River
Cease to flow in sparkling purity
Through the Land of the Divine Wind.

Time: suspension of temporal progression; time is treated as theme
Space: juxtaposition of poems implies that river here flows through plains
 of 28
Motifs: place names, continued; this poem provides a brief but welcome
 change of tone; it harmonizes the concern with time and the past (in
 26–28) by contrasting the transience of ordinary human and natural phe-
 nomena with the permanence of the imperial line; water is associated
 with snows of winter, which ended with 28

LAMENTS

30]   In this mortal world,
Whether we linger on or pass away ahead,
 Our brief span is like
The greater fall of dewdrops from the leaves,
Or the shorter drop of moisture from the stalk.

Time: treatment as theme, continued
Space: progression suspended throughout laments
Motifs: dew and drops of water are associated with river of 29; evanescent
 human life contrasts with stable imperial line of 29; plants-grass imagery
 reintroduced

31]   Minahito wa
Hana no koromo ni
Narinu nari
Koke no tamoto yo
Kawaki dani se yo.

Bishop Henjō. KKS, XVI: 847. "It was at the time of the Fukakusa Emperor when, having been Chief Chamberlain and waited on His Majesty day and night, upon His Majesty's passing away, he renounced all further dealings with the world and, climbing up Mount Hiei, took the tonsure. The next year everyone took off his mourning, and some received caps of promotion to higher rank; there was general rejoicing—whereupon, hearing of all this [Henjō] composed the following."

Koke no tamoto means moss-colored robes worn by priests and also suggests sleeves so wet with tears they have grown mossy.

NSDS 651, EGTG 67

32]   Morotomo ni
Koke no shita ni wa
Kuchizu shite
Uzumorenu na o
Miru zo kanashiki.

Lady Izumi Shikibu (967?–ca. 1040). KYS, X: 660. "After Lady Koshikibu died, ex-Empress Jōtō Mon'in nevertheless sent to the dead lady the present of cloth that she had been accustomed to giving her for years past. Upon examining the cloth and finding the name 'Lady Koshikibu' on it, [Lady Izumi Shikibu] composed the following."

Koshikibu, who died in childbirth (1025), was Izumi Shikibu's daughter. Both had been ladies-in-waiting to Jōtō Mon'in, who sent the present as an unusual mark of affection and sympathy.

NSDS 663, EGTG 68, HDSSI 48

31]   It seems all others
Have changed to robes that blossom flowers:
    Oh, at least allow
Yourselves to dry, my sleeves of moss—
The priestly color and result of tears.

Time: a new temporal progression—a period of mourning—begins with
    this poem and continues through 35; the seasons progress from spring, in
    this poem, to late autumn or early winter in 34
Motifs: mossy sleeves and tears are associated with dew and moisture of 30;
    plants-grass imagery

32]   It remains behind,
Filling me with sorrow at the sight:
    Her unburied name
Did not attend her to the grave
To waste beneath the moss.

Time: period since death increased
Motifs: moss image, continued, here symbolizing passage of time

79

33]　　　　Kagiri areba
　　　　　　Kyō nugisutetsu
　　　　　　Fujigoromo
　　　　　　Hate naki mono wa
　　　　　　Namida narikeri.

Fujiwara Michinobu (972–94). SIS, XX: 1293. "On removing his robes of
mourning for his father, Lord Gōtoku."
Fujigoromo: robes woven of very rough, coarse hempen fiber, worn as a
sign of mourning.
TKJT 131, NSDS 678, EGTG 69, HDSSI 30

34]　　　　Naki hito no
　　　　　　Katami no kumo ya
　　　　　　Shiguru ran
　　　　　　Yūbe no ame ni
　　　　　　Iro wa mienedo.

Go-Toba. SKKS, VIII: 803. "On the topic 'Impermanence in the Rain.'"
This may be an allusion to the *Kao T'ang Fu*, a poem in the *Wen Hsüan*,
which tells of a heavenly maiden from Mount Wu who appeared in a dream
to King Hsiang of Ch'u and promised she would appear as a morning cloud
the next day and in the evening would fall as rain; when the king awoke the
next morning, he saw a cloud trailing in the sky just as she had said; for
this reason, he built a pavilion, which he called the Pavilion of the Morning
Cloud.
NSDS 709, EGTG 71

33]   Custom so decrees,
     And today I have removed my robes
     Of mourning hemp—
     But no arbitrary limit can be set
     To the tears I shed in grief.

Time: end of ritual mourning
Motifs: grief—here the speaker finds its symbol (robe) inadequate; plants-
grass imagery, continued

34]   The cloud from the pyre—
     The last visible keepsake of one now gone—
      Has it turned to drizzle,
     Although its shape cannot be seen
     As it falls mingling with the rain at dusk?

Time: recollection of the dead in late autumn or early winter, the season of
drizzle; end of year begun in 31
Motifs: grief—speaker finds its symbol (cloud of smoke from the pyre) valid,
as in 32, but it vanishes, leaving him, unlike speaker of 32, with no physi-
cal reminder of the dead; rain and drizzle associate with the tears of 33

35]   Kono yo nite
          Mata aumajiki
          Kanashisa ni
          Susumeshi hito zo
          Kokoro midareshi.

Saigyō. szs, IX: 604. A reply to a poem by Jakuren (szs, IX: 603), which
has the headnote, "Sent to Priest Saigyō on hearing that Priest Saijū had
died with his mind composed in the proper fashion."
NSDS 729, HDSSI 62

36]   Tachiwakare
          Inaba no yama no
          Mine ni ouru
          Matsu to shi kikaba
          Ima kaerikon.

Ariwara Yukihira (818–93). KKS, VIII: 365. "Topic unknown."
The poem was presumably addressed to Yukihira's well-wishers at a party
in his honor before he left to take up his post as Governor of Inaba province
in 855. *Inaba* pivots the place name and "where I go." *Matsu* pivots "your
desire for me stays ever green" and "pines."
TKJT 160, NSDS 730, EGTG 72, HNSK 9, HDSSI 5, HNIS 16

35]   In anguished knowledge
       That there can be no further meetings
         In this mortal world,
       The heart of him is turbulent with grief
       Who bade the other face the end with calm.

Time: progression ends
Motifs: death and grief; generalized application of this poem recalls the generalization of first lament (30); the treatment of a specific death, developed from 31–34, concludes here with emphasis on the finality of death

PARTING POEM

36]   Though we part now,
       I shall return the moment I am told
         That, like the pines
       Upon the mountains of Inaba where I go,
       Your desire for me stays ever green.

Time: moment of parting
Space: spatial progression resumed; an imagined journey begins, to be continued through travel and into love poems
Motifs: parting, with a possibility of meeting again; place names reintroduced; -wakare related to au- in 35 by principle of contrasting pairs (meet and part)

37] Wakuraba ni
Tou hito araba
Suma no ura ni
Moshio taretsutsu
Wabu to kotae yo.

Yukihira. KKS, XVIII: 962. "Sent to someone at the Palace when, during the reign of Emperor Montoku, [Yukihira] retired in disgrace to Suma in the province of Tsu."
Moshio taretsutsu pivots "bearing . . . dripping pails" (literally, "pouring seawater on the saltweed") and "spilling . . . upon my sleeves."
 TKJT 18, NSDS 782, EGTG 74, HDSSI 9

38] Naniwabito
Ashihi taku ya ni
Yado karite
Suzuro ni sode no
Shio taruru ran.

Shunzei. SKKS, X: 973. "On 'The Spirit of Travel,' from a sequence of one hundred poems composed at the house of the Lay Priest and Former Chancellor, Tadamichi."
An allusive variation on MYS, XI: 2651, Anonymous.

Naniwabito	She may be as sooty
Ashihi taku ya no	As a hut where the fisherfolk of Naniwa
Sushite aredo	Burn but reeds for fuel,
Ono ga tsuma koso	And yet one's own wife is a treasure
Tsune mezurashiki.	That grows more precious with the passing days.

KSB 24, NSDS 822, EGTG 76

84

37]   If someone should ask,
        Answer that I live in suffering,
          Bearing to the salt kilns
    On the shore of Suma dripping pails,
    Spilling more salt drops upon my sleeves.

Time: journey begins
Space: progression from mountains of 36 to seashore; speaker is at his desti-
    nation but is addressing person left behind
Motifs: place names, continued; ironic contrast of freedom of speaker in 36
    with captivity here; this poem, traditionally classified as "mixed" but re-
    classified by Teika in *Nishidaishū* as "travel," provides transition

38]   Lodging for the night
    In a hut where the fisherfolk of Naniwa
          Burn but reeds for fuel—
    Why does the smoke somehow bring tears,
    Spilling salt drops on the traveler's sleeves?

Time: journey, continued
Space: speaker travels northeast along the coast, as place names show
Motifs: place names, continued; imagery of spilling brine for tears is shared
    with 37 (*moshio taretsutsu* and *shio taruru*)

39]   Tachikaeri
        Mata mo kite min
        Matsushima ya
        Oshima no tomaya
        Nami ni arasu na.

Shunzei. SKKS, X: 933. "A travel poem composed for a sequence of fifty poems at the house of the Cloistered Prince Shukaku."
Oshima is one of hundreds of pine-clad islands in the lovely Matsushima archipelago, celebrated as one of Japan's three most beautiful places. *Tachikaeri* (return) and *nami* (waves) are associated words.

TKJT 249, KSB 25, NSDS 827, EGTG 77, HDSSI 78

40]   Akeba mata
        Koyubeki yama no
        Mine nare ya
        Sora yuku tsuki no
        Sue no shirakumo.

Fujiwara Ietaka (1158–1237). SKKS, X: 939. "When he submitted a sequence of fifty poems."

TKJT 135, NSDS 829, EGTG 78, HDSSI 77

39]   Just as waves return,
        I shall come again to Matsushima
          To gaze on Oshima,
        So do not let the rough seas batter
        The thatch-roofed hut that sheltered me.

Time: journey, continued; day, following night of 38
Space: movement along coast to northeast, continued, but the speaker is
    about to turn inland
Motifs: place names, rude dwelling, and water imagery, continued; loneli-
    ness of travel yields to appreciation of the natural scene

40]   When daylight comes,
        Must I cross yet another mountain peak
          There where white clouds float
        Just beyond the radiant reach of light
        From the moon that journeys through the sky?

Time: journey, continued; night, following day of 39
Space: traveler reaches the mountains
Motifs: contrast of mountains with seacoast of 39; emphasis on the beauty
    of the natural scene, continued; loneliness of travel and appreciation of
    nature are harmonized by the image of the moon traveling through the
    sky

41]   Naniwae no
         Mo ni uzumoruru
         Tamagashiwa
         Arawarete dani
         Hito o koiba ya.

Shunrai. szs, XI: 640. "Composed on 'The Spirit of Beginning Love' for a
sequence of one hundred poems presented at the time of ex-Emperor Hori-
kawa."
The first three lines provide a preface for the last two, with the juncture
at *arawarete* (openly).

NSDS 836, EGTG 79, HDSSI 64

42]   Morasu na yo
         Kumo iru mine no
         Hatsushigure
         Ko no ha wa shita ni
         Iro kawaru to mo.

Fujiwara Yoshitsune. skks, XII: 1087. "On 'The Spirit of Suppressed
Love,' for a contest of hundred-poem sequences at his house when he was
Commander of the Left."
The meaning of this "closed" allegory can be guessed from the headnote
and from the poems preceding and following it here. As the leaves are dyed
by the autumn drizzle, so the speaker's sleeves are dyed by the "tears of
blood" he sheds in unrequited passion.

NSDS 837, EGTG 80

LOVE POEMS

41]   Like the precious rocks
That lie buried underneath the seaweed
In the Bay of Naniwa,
My passion lies buried in my breast—
If only I might love you openly!

Time: Progression of a courtly love affair replaces journey; the transition is made by the place name

Space: travel of preceding sequence becomes a subplot, conveyed by place names and natural imagery; Naniwa was on the coast, southwest of the capital

Motifs: alternation of seacoast and mountain scenes, continued

42]   Do not reveal the sight,
O clouds that hide the mountain peak,
Although beneath you
The leaves be dyed to scarlet
By the first chill autumn rain.

Time: secret love, continued

Space: from seacoast to mountains

Motifs: alternation of seacoast and mountain scenes, continued; the beauty of nature, continued from the later travel poems, functions here allegorically; beginning of subsequence of progressively smaller images, from great stand of trees implied in this poem to reed-joint of 47

43] Azumaji no
Sano no funahashi
Kakete nomi
Omoiwataru o
Shiru hito no naki.

Minamoto Hitoshi (880–951). GSS, X: 620. "Sent to a certain person."
 The first two lines are a preface for the last three, with play on *kakete* (steadfast and spans). *Naki*: emended from *nasa*, in the *Kindai Shūka*, following GSS and *Eiga Taigai*. *Hashi* (bridge) and *-wataru* (spans) are associated words. The Bridge of Sano was in the province of Kōzuke in northeastern Honshu.

NSDS 865, EGTG 81, HDSSI 17

44] Asajifu no
Ono no shinohara
Shinoburedo
Amarite nado ka
Hito no koishiki.

Hitoshi. GSS, IX: 578. "Sent to someone."
 The first two lines are a preface for the last three, with a play on the sounds of *shinohara* and *shinoburedo*.
 The poem appears to be a reworking of KKS, XI: 505, Anonymous.

Asajifu no	Since no one can tell her,
Ono no shinohara	How might she know about my suffering—
Shinobu to mo	When it is a passion
Hito shiru rame ya	I keep as far from sight as small bamboos
Iu hito nashi ni.	Hidden in some patch in grassy fields?

NSDS 869, EGTG 82, HNSK 37, HDSSI 16, HNIS 40

43]   Although it spans
       The great distance that divides us—
         Steadfast and true
       Like the Bridge of Sano to the East—
       My love remains unknown to anyone.

Time: secret love, continued
Space: from mountains to river in implied lowlands
Motifs: development of progressively smaller images

44]   Why does it grow so
       Into a love that swells beyond concealment,
         When it is a passion
       I keep as far from sight as small bamboos
       Hidden in some patch in grassy fields?

Time: secret love, continued; the passion is becoming more uncontrollable
Space: from river to fields
Motifs: progressively smaller images—patch of bamboos follows bridge of 43

45]
Ika ni sen
Muro no Yashima ni
Yado mo ga na
Koi no keburi o
Sora ni magaen.

Shunzei. szs, XI: 702. "On 'Suppressed Love.'"
Muro in Yashima was a lake in Shimotsuke province where the vapor rising from the water was famous for its resemblance to smoke. *Koi* (written *ko-hi* in the Japanese syllabary) pivots *koi* (love) and -*hi* (fire).
KSB 27, NSDS 874, EGTG 83, HDSSI 66

46]
Yūzukuyo
Sasu ya okabe no
Matsu no ha no
Itsu to mo wakanu
Koi mo suru kana.

Anonymous. KKS, XI: 490. "Topic unknown."
Matsu means both "pines" and "waiting." Imagery of evening and waiting suggests a female speaker, but for the present sequence Teika treats the poem as a declaration of steadfast love from the lover to his beloved.
NSDS 890

45]   How can it be borne?
If only I had a dwelling far away
    At Muro in Yashima,
Then might I let the smoke of stifled passion
Tower to the sky for all to see!

Time: secret love has grown unbearable
Space: from river scene in province of Kōzuke (43), across fields (44), to the
   lake of Muro in Yashima in the neighboring province of Shimotsuke
Motifs: further reduction in imagery to a dwelling

46]   My love for you
Is as unvarying in its color
    As the needles of the pines
Waiting on the hillslopes for the moon
To come and bring the splendor of the night.

Time: secret love, continued; passion persists despite lack of encouragement
Space: movement to implied hillside dwelling
Motifs: further reduction in imagery to pine needles; moon associates with
   sky of 45

47]   Naniwagata
        Mijikaki ashi no
        Fushi no ma mo
        Awade kono yo o
        Sugushite yo to ya.

Lady Ise (fl. ca. 935). SKKS, XI: 1049. "Topic unknown."
The first three lines to *ma* form a preface, with a play on *ma* (space and time).

NSDS 909, EGTG 85, HNSK 19, HNIS 19

48]   Ukarikeru
        Hito o Hatsuse no
        Yamaoroshi yo
        Hageshikare to wa
        Inoranu mono o.

Shunrai. SZS, XII: 707. "On the spirit of 'Love for a Person Who Will not Vouchsafe a Meeting Despite One's Prayers to the Gods,' when he composed ten poems on love at the house of the Acting Middle Counselor Toshitada."
    At Hatsuse in Yamato province was the popular Hase Temple, dedicated to the Buddhist divinity Kannon. She was believed to favor star-crossed lovers. In the "version sent away," Teika writes "[This poem has] deep feeling, the words freely following the flow of the sentiment, ... truly an effect that is difficult to achieve."

TKJT 188, KSB 10, NSDS 933, EGTG 86, HDSSI 67, HNIS 74

94

47]   Without a meeting,
Though it be short as a joint of reed
In the marshes of Naniwa—
Is this the kind of loveless life
That you are urging me to lead?

Time: lover remonstrates with the reluctant lady
Space: from hills of 46 to tidal marshes of Naniwa; end of a westerly pro-
gression from Yashima in 45 to places near the capital
Motifs: conclusion of subsequence of diminishing images with the reed-
joint; *matsu* (pine and wait) in 46 is related to *awade* (without a meet-
ing); subsequence of place names begins and continues through 54

48]   Your cold disfavor
Blows like the storm that rages down
From the mountain of Hatsuse,
Although my prayer at that sacred shrine
Was not that your cruelty be increased!

Time: period of woman's rejection continues, while lover is seeking means
to overcome it
Space: from flats of Naniwa in 47 due east to base of mountains in Hatsuse,
south of the capital
Motifs: contrast of great mountain image with the series of diminishing
images that ended with 47

49]   Omoigawa
            Taezu nagaruru
            Mizu no awa no
            Utakata hito ni
            Awade kieme ya.

Lady Ise. GSS, IX: 516. "Once when she had gone off with a certain person without telling anyone, another man with whom she was on intimate terms sent word that he had been making inquiries about her for many days in great distress, thinking that she had disappeared forever, whereupon she composed the following."

Omoigawa (Stream of Love) is said to have been the name of a river in the province of Chikuzen (Kyushu). The first three lines form a preface for the last two, with a play on *utakata* (foam and utterly). The two sections are also joined by word association between *awa* (foam) and *kieme* (vanish), as well as by the echo of *awa* in *awade*.

TKJT 4, NSDS 935, EGTG 88, HDSSI 15

50]   Naki na nomi
            Tatsu no ichi to wa
            Sawagedo mo
            Isa mata hito o
            Uru yoshi mo nashi.

Attributed to Hitomaro. SIS, XII: 700. "Topic unknown."

Tatsu pivots the place name and "rise." *Uru* means both "obtain" and "sell"; in the second sense it is an associated word with *ichi* (market).

TKJT 205, NSDS 951, EGTG 89

49]   Without a meeting,
         Could I, like the insubstantial foam
           Flowing ceaselessly
        In the current of the Stream of Love,
        Vanish utterly from your sight?

Time: lady encourages lover to continue his suit
Space: leap from Hatsuse to river in Chikuzen
Motifs: river associated with the mountains of 48 (rivers conventionally
   originate in mountains)

50]   For all those rumors,
        Rising like the vendors' lying cries
          In the Tatsu market,
        I have yet to discover how
        To strike a bargain with this girl.

Time: the lover's success is rumored, but he has not yet found a way to gain
   access to the lady
Space: return leap from Chikuzen to the Yamato area south of the capital;
   both here and in 49 the sudden change of direction stresses the difference
   between appearance and reality

51]   Yura no to o
        Wataru funabito
        Kaji o tae
        Yukue mo shiranu
        Koi no michi kana.

Sone no Yoshitada (fl. ca. 985). SKKS, XI: 1071. "Topic unknown."
The first four lines form a preface for the fifth, with the juncture at
shiranu (does not know). *Yukue* (journey's end) and *michi* (course) are asso-
ciated words with *funabito* (boatman).

NSDS 967, HNSK 47, HNIS 46

52]   Karakoromo
        Sode ni hitome wa
        Tsutsumedo mo
        Moreizuru mono wa
        Namida narikeri.

Fujiwara Koretada (924–72). SKKS, XI: 1003. "Sent to a woman on some
unknown occasion."
Moreizuru: the SKKS text gives *koboruru*, but the difference in meaning is
slight.

NSDS 976

98

51]   The course of love:
In crossing the perilous waters
    Of the Straits of Yura,
The boatman who has lost his rudder
And does not know his journey's end.

Time: the progression is suspended (for this poem only) for a general com-
ment on love, summing up what has happened and anticipating what
follows
Space: from inland location to nearby western coast (the Yura Straits are
located between the Isle of Awaji and the Kii Peninsula)

52]   Though I enfold
My suffering in the crimson sleeve
    Of my Chinese gown,
The tears spill out from underneath,
Betraying the secret of my love.

Time: lover renews his appeal
Space: sea voyage continued to Cathay (*Kara-*)
Motifs: tears related to sea imagery of 51; Chinese robes are conventionally
crimson, the color expressing both flames of passion and tears of blood
coloring the sleeve

53]   Takasago no
        Onoe no matsu o
        Fuku kaze no
        Oto ni nomi ya wa
        Kikiwataru kana.

Fujiwara Akisuke (1090–1155). szs, XI: 651. "Composed as a love poem for a sequence of one hundred poems submitted to His Majesty."

The Onoe Shrine at Takasago in Harima province was celebrated for a famous pine tree whose spirit was mystically wedded to the spirit of another pine at Suminoe, suggesting conjugal fidelity and longevity. The first three lines form a preface for the last two, with the juncture at *oto* (sound). The szs reads *ni* for *o* in line 2 and *beki* for *kana* in line 5; the *Nishidaishū* and the "version sent away" also have *beki* in line 5. The meaning is not significantly different.

KSB 14, NSDS 986

54]   Oto ni kiku
        Takashi no hama no
        Adanami wa
        Kakeji ya sode no
        Nure mo koso sure.

Lady Kii (fl. ca. 1100). KYS, VIII: 501. This poem is the reply in an exchange with Fujiwara Toshitada, "Composed for a contest of lovers' poetic exchanges at the time of ex-Emperor Horikawa."

This match of gallant poetic exchanges is the only such contest of which the poems survive.

NSDS 987, HNSK 74, HDSSI 47, HNIS 72

53]   How can I go on
Loving you only through what I hear—
      Faint rumors of you
Like the wind that whispers in the pines
Of Onoe on Takasago's shore?

Time: lover's appeal, continued
Space: return from Cathay to Japanese coast
Motifs: the very Japanese associations of Takasago (in Harima) contrast
  with the exotic gown of 52

54]   Having heard so much
Of those capricious waves that beat along
      Your shore of Takashi,
I shall take care lest they give my sleeves
Cause to be wetted with a spray of tears.

Time: the lady begins to relent, taxing her suitor with his reputation for
  fickleness but offering some hope
Space: movement eastward up the coast from Harima to Settsu province
Motifs: resumption of clothes imagery from 52; *oto ni kiku* is similar to
  oto ni nomi . . . kiki- (53); place names subsequence concluded

101

55]   Tsutsumedo mo
Kakurenu mono wa
Natsumushi no
Mi yori amareru
Omoi narikeri.

Anonymous. GSS, IV: 209. "When commanded by Princess Katsura to catch her some fireflies, someone presented them to her wrapped in the sleeve of a little girl's summer robe, together with this poem."

Omoi (written *omohi* in the Japanese syllabary; cf. 45, above) pivots *omoi* (love) and *omo-hi* (great fire). The poem is classified as a summer poem in GSS; in the *Yamato Monogatari*, however, a young woman in Princess Katsura's entourage addressed the poem to Prince Shikibu-kyō when she was enamored of him, even though he was the Princess's lover.

TKJT 58, NSDS 995, HDSSI 11

56]   Kataito o
Konata kanata ni
Yorikakete
Awazuba nani o
Tama no o ni sen.

Sakanoue Korenori. KKS, XI: 483. "Topic unknown."

The first three lines form a preface to the last two, with the juncture at *awazuba* (if we cannot meet).

NSDS 1022, EGTG 90

55]   Though folded in a robe,
The fireflies still burst forth in flames
    That cannot be concealed—
Like the fiery passion that I bear you,
Bursting forth from out my very flesh.

Time: the lover replies, intensifying his appeal
Space: a new progression is begun, moving from the outdoors to the do-
  mestic scene suggested by the robe
Motifs: clothes imagery, continued; water (54) and fire metaphorically con-
  trast lady's coldness and lover's ardor

56]   If we cannot meet,
Joining together like the threads I twine
    Now so, then thus,
To make a cord to string my jewels upon,
Of what shall I make up my thread of life?

Time: the lady declares her love
Space: movement indoors
Motifs: jewels and threads are associated with clothes images of preceding
  poems; emphasis on the small and personal here and in 57

57]   Omoigusa
Hazue ni musubu
Shiratsuyu no
Tamatama kite wa
Te ni mo tamarazu.

Shunrai. KYS, VII: 444. "On the topic, 'The Lover Comes but Does Not Stay,' when people were composing ten poems on love at the house of Lord Toshitada."
The first three lines form a preface for the last two, with *tamatama* pivoting "bejeweling" and "at last." The witty repetition of sounds in the last two lines has often been noted. In the "version sent away," Teika praises this poem as "the work of a skilled poet."

    KSB 9, NSDS 1036, EGTG 91, HDSSI 46

58]   Omoiki ya
Shiji no hashigaki
Kakitsumete
Momoyo mo onaji
Marone sen to wa.

Shunzei. SZS, XII: 778. "Composed on the spirit of 'A Love Promise Broken on the Promised Night,' at a poetry contest in the palace of the Hōjūji ex-Emperor."
Shunzei's poem is based on a legend about a lady who tested her suitor by commanding him to sleep a hundred nights on his carriage rest outside her door before she would yield to him. The lover came for ninety-nine nights, cutting a notch on his carriage rest each time, but on the hundredth day his father died, making his visit impossible. The lady sends him a poem saying that since he has not come she will have to cut a notch on the carriage rest herself.

    KSB 26, NSDS 1037, EGTG 92

57]   Like the white dew
Bejeweling leaf tips of the passion flowers
    But fleeing from the grasp,
You do at last make precious one brief hour
Only to leave just as my hands would take you in.

Time: the lady reproaches the lover for his merely perfunctory visits; early
   evening, since the lover does not stay
Space: transition to outdoors
Motifs: *tamatama* echoes the *tama* of 56; the jewels of 56 are here treated
   as the dew

58]   Could I have thought it—
To be, even on the hundredth night,
    Condemned as on the others
To cut upon my carriage rest a notch
And sleep in my own clothes outside your door?

Time: the lover is rebuffed by the angry lady; passing of the night
Space: from the garden the lover addresses the lady within (pretending he
   has now visited her in vain for the hundredth time)
Motifs: diction in the first lines and alliteration in the last two are similar
   in 57 and 58

59]   Ariake no
        Tsurenaku mieshi
        Wakare yori
        Akatsuki bakari
        Uki mono wa nashi.

Mibu no Tadamine. KKS, XIII: 625. "Topic unknown."
TKJT 6, NSDS 1070, EGTG 93, HNSK 24, HDSSI 7, HNIS 30

60]   Samushiro ni
        Koromo katashiki
        Koyoi mo ya
        Ware o matsu ran
        Uji no hashihime.

Anonymous. KKS, XIV: 689. "Topic unknown."
The lover treats his beloved as if she were the Lady of the Uji Bridge, a
kind of guardian deity.
TKJT 164, NSDS 1081

59]   Since that parting,
     When your indifference was as cold
      As the fading moon at dawn,
   I have known no kind of wretchedness
   Like that brought by the break of day.

Time: the lover writes, reproaching the lady for her cruelty; dawn follow-
   ing the night of 58
Space: departure from the lady's garden
Motifs: imagery of moon and dawn follows night of 58

60]   On her mat of straw
   Does the Lady of the Bridge of Uji
      Once again tonight
   Spread out her half-folded garment
   And lie there waiting, expecting me to come?

Time: the lover, having decided to abandon the affair, wonders whether
   the lady expects him to visit her as usual
Space: the lover, at a distance, imagines the situation at the lady's house
Motifs: continued emphasis upon the time of day—tonight (*koyoi*) con-
   trasts with dawn (*akatsuki*) of 59

61]   Natorigawa
        Seze no umoregi
        Arawareba
        Ika ni sen to ka
        Aimisomeken.

Anonymous. KKS, XIII: 650. "Topic unknown."
The first two lines form a preface for the last three, with the juncture at
arawareba (reveal and rise to view). *Natorigawa* (Scandal River) is the
name of a river in northern Honshu.

NSDS 1090, EGTG 94, HDSSI 8

62]   Ima kon to
        Iishi bakari ni
        Nagatsuki no
        Ariake no tsuki o
        Machiidetsuru kana.

Sosei. KKS, XIV: 691. "Topic unknown."
The situation shows that Sosei intended the speaker to be a woman.
Nagatsuki (Long Moon) is the ninth month in the lunar year.

TKJT 31, NSDS 1105, EGTG 95, HNSK 22, HNIS 21

61]   What did I mean to do
        When first I lay down by your side,
          If our secret were revealed—
        As on the currents of Scandal a sunken log
        May rise suddenly to shameful view?

Time: the lady fears the loss of her reputation and, now that the lover has
  grown indifferent, regrets having entered upon the affair; night, by in-
  ference from preceding poem
Space: return to lady's house
Motifs: association of currents (*seze*) and the river with the bridge of 60

62]   Although you said
        That you would come to me at once,
          I have waited for you
        Throughout the Long Moon's longest night
        Until the moon at dawn waned in the sky.

Time: lady waits in vain as her lover's indifference grows; dawn
Space: indoors situation, continued; the lady contemplates the outdoors

109

63]   Au koto wa
            Tōyamazuri no
            Karigoromo
            Kite wa kai naki
            Ne o nomi zo naku.

Prince Motonaga (901–76). GSS, X: 680. "On receiving the present of a hunting costume from a lady whom he was secretly visiting."

The text of the second line has been emended from *tōyamadori no* (the fowl of distant mountains) to *tōyamazuri no* (stenciled with a pattern of distant mountains), in accordance with GSS and *Eiga Taigai*. *Kite* in line 4 pivots "wear" and "come to you."

NSDS 1121, EGTG 96, HDSSI 18

64]   Ashihiki no
            Yamadori no o no
            Shidario no
            Naganagashi yo o
            Hitori ka mo nen.

Attributed to Hitomaro. SIS, XIII: 778. "Topic unknown."

Ashihiki no (footsore): pillow-word for *yama-* (hills, mountains). The first three lines form a preface for the last two with the juncture at *naganagashi* (long).

NSDS 1122, EGTG 97, SKDT 93, HNSK 3, HDSSI 26, HNIS 3

63]   The time we meet
      Must be as distant as the painted mountains
        On this hunting cloak:
      To wear it to you would bring no real game,
      Only my voice a cause for futile cries.

Time: the lover writes, acknowledging the lady's attempt to reestablish
    their relationship but disingenuously excusing himself; day, following the
    dawn of 62
Space: return to lover's surroundings
Motifs: association of moon in 62 with distant mountains; focus on out-
    doors, continued

64]   Must I sleep alone
      All through the long, long night,
        Long as the tail,
      The flowing tail of the mountain fowl
      Dwelling in the footsore hills?

Time: the abandoned lady appeals for a resumption of the affair in answer
    to her lover's accusation; dusk
Space: return to the lady's surroundings for rest of love sequence; subpro-
    gression from mountains here to mountains of 70 begins
Motifs: wild fowl associates with hunting cloak and game of 63; outdoors
    and mountain imagery, continued

65]   Wabinureba
        Ima hata onaji
        Na ni wa naru
        Mi o tsukushite mo
        Awan to zo omou.

Prince Motonaga. GSS, XIII: 961. SIS, XII: 766. "Sent to the Kyōgoku Lady of the Bedchamber after their affair became known."
    The lady becomes the speaker in Teika's sequence. *Na ni wa naru* pivots "name grow common" with *Naniwa naru,* "of Naniwa." *Mi o tsukushite mo* pivots "risk my life" and *miotsukushi,* "channel markers."

TKJT 1, NSDS 1205, EGTG 98, HNSK 20, HDSSI 25, HNIS 20

66]   Sumiyoshi no
        Kishi ni yoru nami
        Yoru sae ya
        Yume no kayoiji
        Hitome yoku ran.

Fujiwara Toshiyuki (d. 901). KKS, XII: 559. "A poem for the poetry contest at the Palace of the Empress in the Kampei era."
    The first two lines form a preface for the last three, with the juncture at *yoru,* which pivots "visiting" (of the waves to the shore) and "night." KKS reads *Suminoe* for the first line, but the two words are merely different names for the same place.

NSDS 1219, HNSK 10, HNIS 18

65]   I live in a wretchedness
        That makes me need to see you yet again—
        Though my name once more
        Grow common as the channel markers of Naniwa
        And the risk I run be that of life itself.

Time: the lady desperately appeals for renewed intimacy, expressing will-
    ingness to risk the scandal she had feared
Space: movement in subprogression from mountains to seashore
Motifs: water imagery

66]   Though waves are safe
        In visiting the shores of Sumiyoshi,
            Must I be denied
        Even your dream visits in the night,
        As you avoid men's eyes along that path?

Time: the lady writes, pleading for the lover's consideration: not only has
    he discontinued his visits, but she cannot dream of him, which shows
    that he has ceased even to think of her; to provide him with an excuse
    for his neglect, she attributes it to fear of scandal
Space: further west along the coast of the Inland Sea
Motifs: water imagery, continued

67]   Koi seji to
        Mitarashigawa ni
        Seshi misogi
        Kami wa ukezu mo
        Narinikeru kana.

Anonymous. KKS, XI: 501. "Topic unknown."
KKS text for last two lines, *Kami wa ukezu zo / Narinikerashi mo,* is some-
what more emphatic in the fourth, and slightly less in the fifth, lines.
NSDS has *mo / -kerashi mo.*

NSDS 1243

68]   Chigiriki na
        Katami ni sode o
        Shiboritsutsu
        Sue no matsuyama
        Nami kosaji to wa.

Kiyowara Motosuke (908–90). GSIS, XIV: 770. "Composed for someone to
send to a woman whose feelings had changed."
An allusive variation on KKS, XX: 1093, Anonymous.

Kimi o okite   If I should ever
Adashigokoro o   Cast you aside, if you discover mine
    Waga motaba   A fickle woman's heart,
Sue no matsuyama   May the waves rise up and flood
Nami mo koenan.   The tops of pines upon Mount Sue!

NSDS 1316, EGTG 102, HNSK 45, HDSSI 37, HNIS 42

67]   With ritual cleansing
        In the purifying river, I declared,
          "I will love no more."
        But the vow appeared to be displeasing
        To the gods, who sent me back denied.

Time: convinced that she cannot regain her lover, the lady tries unsuccess-
    fully to put him from her thoughts
Space: from seacoast of 66 to river
Motifs: water imagery, continued

68]   To think you vowed,
        As we wrung out our tear-soaked sleeves
            In symbol of our troth,
        That the waves would never rise to flood
        The tops of pines upon Mount Sue!

Time: alluding to the curse in an old poem (translated opposite), the lady
    renews her reproaches
Space: movement northward and inland
Motifs: water imagery, continued

69] Mi-Kumano no
Ura yori ochi ni
Kogu fune no
Ware oba yoso ni
Hedatetsuru kana.

Lady Ise. skks, XI: 1048. "Topic unknown."
nsds 1319

70] Miwa no yama
Ika ni machimin
Toshi fu to mo
Tazunuru hito mo
Araji to omoeba.

Lady Ise. kks, XV: 780. "Sent to Lord Nakahira Ason, from whom she had become estranged, as she was about to depart for the residence of her father, the Governor of Yamato."
The poem alludes to kks, XVIII: 982, Anonymous.

Waga io wa	My little house
Miwa no yamamoto	Lies at the foot of Miwa mountain—
Koishikuba	If you're fond of me,
Toburaikimase	Why not come and visit with me there?
Sugi tateru kado.	(You can tell it by the cedar at the gate.)

nsds 1344

116

69]   You have drawn away,
        Setting me at an ever greater distance,
           Like a ship that rows
        Far out upon the open sea
        From the bay shore of Kumano.

Time: with no hope of reestablishing their relationship, the lady continues
   her reproaches
Space: movement southwest to the coast of Kumano on the Kii Peninsula,
   south of the capital
Motifs: water imagery, continued

70]   How can I continue
        Waiting at the foot of Miwa mountain,
           Knowing as I do
        That even though the years pass by
        You will never come to visit me?

Time: the lady fears that she cannot long survive her lover's betrayal
Space: from the seacoast of 69 to the mountains in the province of Yamato,
   south of the capital
Motifs: waiting is associated with the sea journey of 69; lady waits in both
   poems; the voyaging lover's return is despaired of

71]   Sode no tsuyu mo
Aranu iro ni zo
   Kiekaeru
Utsureba kawaru
Nageki seshi ma ni.

Go-Toba. skks, XIV: 1323. "On the spirit of 'Forgotten Love.'"
An allusive variation on poem 6 above.
nsds 1288, hdssi 79

72]   Omoiide yo
Ta ga kanegoto no
   Sue naran
Kinō no kumo no
Ato no yamakaze.

Ietaka. skks, XIV: 1294. "For the Poetry Contest in 1,500 Rounds."
tkjt 284, nsds 1357

71]   The dew upon my sleeve
       Changes color to the crimson of despair:
         These tears of my life
       Fade toward death with unavailing sighs
       For that changeful heart that wrought my
           change.

Time: the lady grows weak with bitter resentment, despair, and misery, and weeps tears of blood
Space: subprogression is ended
Motifs: both 70 and 71 are allusive variations

72]   Remember well!
       Whose promises of love were they
         That bring my end?—
       Mere clouds of yesterday blown away
       At the first cold breath of the mountain wind.

Time: the lady sends her lover one last reproach, comparing his vows to fragile clouds dispersed by the wind
Motifs: with sequence drawing to a close, imagery diminishes in importance, and our attention is focused on the lady's emotions

73]　　　Nageke tote
　　　　Tsuki ya wa mono o
　　　　Omowasuru
　　　　Kakochigao naru
　　　　Waga namida kana.

Saigyō. szs, XV: 926. "Composed on the spirit of 'Love Before the Moon.'"
NSDS 1365, EGTG 103, HNSK 88, HDSSI 68, HNIS 86

74]　　　Kuma mo naki
　　　　Ori shi mo hito o
　　　　Omoiidete
　　　　Kokoro to tsuki o
　　　　Yatsushitsuru kana.

Saigyō. SKKS, XIV: 1268. "Topic unknown."
In Saigyō's personal collection, the Sankashū, the headnote says "On 'Love Before the Moon.'"
NSDS 1370, HDSSI 80

73]   Is it possible,
Could the moon have said, "Lament!"
    That it should arouse
A cast of bitterness upon my face
And cause these anguished tears to flow?

Time: attempting to resign herself and to seek consolation in gazing at the
   beauty of the moon, the lady finds that it reawakens thoughts of the lover
Motifs: moon is associated with clouds and mountain of 72

74]   I remembered him
Just as its bright light emerged
    Into a cloudless sky,
And the weakness of my heart brought tears
That blurred the radiance of the moon.

Time: sometime later the lady is again reminded of her former lover by
   the moon, and the memory arouses feelings of sadness and regret; end of
   love sequence
Motifs: moon image, continued; the softened tone contrasts with the bit-
   terness of 73

75]   Saga no yama
           Miyuki taenishi
             Serigawa no
           Chiyo no furumichi
           Ato wa arikeri.

Yukihira. GSS, XV: 1076. "Composed on the day Emperor Kōkō made an Imperial Excursion to the Seri River, reviving the practice established by Emperor Saga."

Saga plays on the place name and the name of the former emperor. *Miyuki* means both "Imperial Excursion" and "deep snow." *Furu-* means both "ancient" and "fall," and associates with *miyuki* (deep snow) in the second sense. *Ato* means both "unchanged" and "footprints," and in the latter sense associates with the first meaning of *miyuki* (Imperial Excursion) and with *taenishi* (disappeared, i.e., as of footprints) and *-michi* (path).

NSDS 1449, SKDT 108, HDSSI 19

76]   Okitsukaze
           Fukinikerashi na
             Sumiyoshi no
           Matsu no shizue o
           Arau shiranami.

Tsunenobu. GSIS, XVIII: 1064. "Composed when about to return from an Imperial Pilgrimage to Sumiyoshi in the third month of 1073."

An allusive variation upon KKS, VII: 360, by Ōshikōchi Mitsune.

Suminoe no	With the autumn wind
Matsu o akikaze	Blowing through the ageless pines
Fuku kara ni	Of auspicious Suminoe
Koe uchisouru	Are mingled the elated voices
Okitsu shiranami.	Of the white waves out to sea.

KSB 3, NSDS 1452, HDSSI 40

MIXED TOPICS

Congratulatory

75]   On Saga Mountain
       The deep snows have disappeared today,
         And the Imperial path
       Leading to the Seri River is revealed
       Unchanged throughout a thousand years.

Time: a new sequence, relating the life of a courtier, begins auspiciously
   here, with the tone heightened by spring's arrival and by the courtier's
   receiving the honor of accompanying the emperor
Space: spatial progression resumes; the Seri River was a short distance west
   of the capital
Motifs: marked change in tone from the love sequence; the mountain is as-
   sociated with the moon of 74

76]   It looks as if the wind
       Is blowing off the sea upon the strand
         Of auspicious Sumiyoshi,
       Because white waves come in and wash
       The lower branches of the pines.

Time: courtier continues to enjoy imperial favor; late spring
Space: the journey continues westward to Sumiyoshi, the location of the
   god of longevity and poetry
Motifs: whiteness of waves related to snow in 75; water imagery, continued

77]   Amatsukaze
        Kumo no kayoiji
        Fukitoji yo
        Otome no sugata
        Shibashi todomen.

Bishop Henjō. ĸĸs, XVII: 872. "Composed upon seeing the Gosechi
Dancers."
The Gosechi festival took place in the eleventh month of the lunar calen-
dar. The speaker treats the dancers as celestial beings come down to dance
briefly on earth.

NSDS 1455, HNSK 15, HNIS 12

78]   Chigiri okishi
        Sasemo ga tsuyu o
        Inochi nite
        Aware kotoshi no
        Aki mo inumeri.

Fujiwara Mototoshi (d. 1142). szs, XVI: 1023. "When Bishop Kōkaku had
often been passed over as Reader at the Vimalakīrti Ceremony, [his father]
complained to . . . Lord Tadamichi and received the reply 'The fields of
Shimeji' [a reference to a poem attributed to the Buddhist divinity Kan-
non]; when [his son] was passed over again the next year, he sent this poem"
—also an allusion to the poem attributed to Kannon (sĸĸs, XX: 1917).

Nao tanome   Trust in me yet,
Shimeji ga hara no   As long as I am here to bless the world,
  Sasemogusa   For my power cures pain
Waga yo no naka ni   Worse than the burning of all the moxa plants
Aran kagiri wa.   That grow on the fields of Shimeji.

ĸsB 20, NSDS 1489, HNSK 82, HDSSI 69, HNIS 75

124

77]   O winds of heaven
        Blow a barrier of clouds across the path
          By which they came,
        That for a moment I may keep in view
        The forms of the Maidens of the Sky!

Time: courtier continues his successful career; gallantry suggests youthful
happiness; return to human activities, as in 75, suggests passage of time;
winter
Space: return to the capital implied by glimpse of Court dancing
Motifs: similar treatment of wind in 76 and 77; clouds associate with white-
ness of waves in 76

Personal Grievances

78]   Depending for my life
        On a promise fragile as the dew
          Upon the moxa plants,
        Alas, the autumn of this year
        Has left me once again with broken hopes.

Time: autumn; an indefinite period of time, perhaps several years, has
elapsed, bringing the courtier unhappiness and disappointment in his
career
Space: from the capital, implied in 77, to provincial fields where moxa
grows (in the eastern province of Shimotsuke)
Motifs: contrast of the moment of beauty in 77 with this long period of
misery; *chigiri* (promise) is used both for vows of love and for more gen-
eral promises, thus linking overtones of love in 77 and emphasis upon
career in 78 and 79

79]   Nagaraeba
Mata kono koro ya
Shinobaren
Ushi to mishi yo zo
Ima wa koishiki.

Kiyosuke. sᴋᴋs, XVIII: 1843. "Topic unknown."
In his personal collection, the *Kiyosuke Ason Shū*, this poem has the fol-
lowing headnote: "Sent to the Sanjō Great Counselor, Fujiwara Kinnori,
when he was still a Middle Commander and I was reminded of the past."

   ᴛᴋᴊᴛ 96, ᴋsʙ 18, ɴsᴅs 1559, ʜɴsᴋ 84, ʜɴɪs 84

80]   Sumiwabiba
Mi o kakusubeki
Yamazato ni
Amari kuma naki
Yowa no tsuki kana.

Shunzei. szs, XVI: 985. "On the spirit of 'A Mountain Dwelling in the
Moonlight.'"
In the "version sent away" and szs, the first line reads *sumiwabite*.
An allusive variation on a poem by Narihira in *Ise Monogatari*.

Sumiwabinu	I am tired of life—
Ima wa kagiri to	Let me seek some secluded dwelling
Yamazato ni	In a mountain village,
Mi o kakusubeki	Where I may hide myself and wait
Yado motometen.	For the end that soon will come.

   ᴛᴋᴊᴛ 121, ᴋsʙ 23, ɴsᴅs 1605

79]   If I live on,
         Perhaps I shall recall with yearning
           This present sadness,
         As I now look back with tenderness
         On days that seemed but wretched at the time.

Time: his failure to advance leads the speaker to reflect on his experience,
   and he achieves some degree of understanding; probably autumn
Space: country implied by the poem's position in the sequence
Motifs: *nagaraeba* (if I live on) is associated with *inochi* (life) of 78

80]   Worn out with living,
           I had thought this mountain village
             To be a safe retreat—
           But it casts a too searching radiance
           In a cloudless sky, this midnight moon.

Time: the speaker has grown older and more careworn; autumn implied by
   bright moon
Space: the speaker withdraws from the capital to a mountain retreat in
   search of peace, but the world's attractions pursue him
Motifs: diction in first line similar to that of 79

81]   Ta ga misogi
       Yūtsukedori ka
       Karakoromo
       Tatsuta no yama ni
       Orihaete naku.

Anonymous. KKS, XVIII: 995. "Topic unknown."
Karakoromo (like a Chinese robe) is a pillow-word for Tatsuta (the mountains of Tatsuta; *tatsu-* means "cut"). *Ori-* (weave) associates with *-koromo* (robe) and *tatsu-*. It is believed that in the ceremony referred to here streamers were attached to fowl, which were released to carry off with them the impurities of a person undergoing purification.

NSDS 1651, HDSSI 10

82]   Kore ya kono
       Yuku mo kaeru mo
       Wakaretsutsu
       Shiru mo shiranu mo
       Ōsaka no seki.

Sosei. GSS, XV: 1090. "On watching the passersby when he was living in a hut that he had built at the Ōsaka Barrier."
The poem has been traditionally regarded as an allegory on karma, rebirth, and the instability of human life and relationships. *Ōsaka* (written *au saka*) pivots the place name and *au* (meet).

NSDS 1654, HNSK 16, HDSSI 20, HNIS 10

Autumn

81]   For whose purification
Was the cock that crows unceasingly
      Bedecked with streamers
Here in the mountains of Tatsuta,
Woven with beauties like a Chinese robe?

Time: the attractions of the world draw the speaker from his retreat, and
   he begins his return journey; mention of Tatsuta, renowned for its au-
   tumn foliage, indicates continuation of autumn; dawn (cockcrow) fol-
   lowing night of 80
Space: movement from the retreat to Tatsuta, site of an ancient barrier or
   military check-point, where he hears a domestic fowl and imagines the
   activities of human beings
Motifs: mountain imagery, continued

Buddhism

82]   Here it is, yes here,
Where these set forth and those return
      And others come to part—
Both friends and strangers meet together
At the Barrier Post of Meeting!

Time: back in the world of men, the speaker likens the busy flux of human
   life he observes there to the wheel of karma and implies a desire to re-
   treat again; autumn, inferred from poem's position in sequence; midday
   following dawn of 81
Space: speaker has moved back toward the capital—from the retreat,
   through the Tatsuta Barrier, to the Barrier of Meeting near the capital's
   southeastern boundary
Motifs: place names; the presence of human beings implied in 81 becomes
   emphatic here

83]   Yo no naka yo
Michi koso nakere
Omoiiru
Yama no oku ni mo
Shika zo naku naru.

Shunzei. szs, XVII: 1148. "Composed as a poem on deer when he wrote a sequence of one hundred poems on 'Expressing Personal Grievances.'" *Omoiiru* pivots "overcome by care" and *-iru* (to which I fled).
KSB 22, NSDS 1710, HNSK 87, HDSSI 70, HNIS 83

Personal Grievances

83]   O wretched world,
        That affords no pathway to release!
          Even the mountain depths
        To which I fled when overcome by care
        Echo with the anguished cry of deer.

Time: the speaker retreats again, but discovers that there is no escape in
    this world from the sorrows of human existence; autumn, implied by cry
    of deer
Space: the speaker has returned to his mountain retreat
Motifs: the religious allegory of 82 is echoed by the first line; the pathway
    (*michi*) associates with the road through the Ōsaka Barrier-Post

APPENDIX

Manuscripts and Versions of the Kindai Shūka

The two versions of the *Kindai Shūka* are known as the *kensō-bon* or "manuscript sent away" (that is, to Sanetomo) and the *ji-hitsubon* or "holograph." They differ in the number, selection, provenance, and order of poems. For several reasons, especially the fact that only the holograph contains the introductory sentence, "This is now a thing of the distant past," there is little doubt that the manuscript sent away is the earlier version.

Typically, neither version originally bore a title. The name *Kindai Shūka* later became traditional for both, although apparent references to the Prefatory Essay or the exemplary poems in the writings of later medieval poets and critics show that various designations for the version sent to Sanetomo were once current. For example, it is presumably this version which Teika's grandson Genshō called "the epistle to the East of the Jōgen era [1207–11]"[1] and which the famous *renga* poet and critic Nijō Yoshimoto (1320–88) called the *"Kinrai Shūka,* written down and sent to the Kamakura Minister of the Right [Sanetomo] by the Kyōgoku Lay Priest Middle Counselor [Teika]."[2] *Superior Poems of Our Time* is an apt description of

[1] Genshō, *Waka Kuden* (or *Gukanshō*), in *NKGT*, IV, 32.
[2] Yoshimoto's designation differs from the traditional title only in the second character. The character for "come" is substituted for the character

the twenty-seven poems sent to Sanetomo, which were all by poets of a generation or two before Teika. This title might never have been applied to the holograph, however, except that it, like the version sent away, contains the Prefatory Essay. Moreover, it is possible, as Professor Hisamatsu believes, that the holograph may once have contained not only the Prefatory Essay and Teika's new sequence of eighty-three poems, but also the poems of the version sent away. Although this seems to us a rather remote possibility, it is suggested by the fact that in a manuscript called the *Hibishō* (Ultra-Secret Notes) the poems of the version sent away, the poems of the holograph, and the Prefatory Essay are found together.[3] Not wishing to further complicate an already confused situation, we have retained the traditional title.

A copy in Teika's own hand of the version sent away is not extant, but it can be dated with reasonable accuracy. A colophon by Teika's son Tameie, preserved in several later manuscript copies, states that the original was sent to the shogun Sanetomo in the Jōgen era. This evidence is corroborated by an entry in the chronicle *Azuma Kagami* (Mirror of the East) for the third year of Jōgen (1209) that refers to poems sent to Teika by Sanetomo: "The poems that had been sent to the Kyōgoku

---

for "era" or "generation." The substitution does not, however, significantly alter the meaning. Nijō Yoshimoto, *Gumon Kenchū*, in *NKGT*, V, 125.

[3] Hisamatsu Sen'ichi, *Chūsei Wakashi (Wakashi,* Vol. III), p. 97. We agree with the late Professor Kazamaki in regarding the eighty-three poems of the holograph as an entirely new formulation by Teika, intended to replace, not supplement, the twenty-seven poems of the version sent away. (See Kazamaki Keijirō, "Fujiwara Teika ni yotte haaku sareta mono," *Nihon Bungakushi no Kenkyū*, I, 358–59.) The version sent away is found, sometimes separately, sometimes along with other essays, in manuscripts bearing a variety of titles: *Wakashiki (Teika-kyō)* (Poetic Precepts [Lord Teika]); *Teika Wakashiki* (Teika's Poetic Precepts); *Jōgen Wakashiki* (Poetic Precepts of the Jōgen Era); *Jōgenshō* (Notes of the Jōgen Era); *Chūnagon Nyūdō (Teika-kyō) Kuden* (Secret Traditions of the Lay Priest Middle Counselor [Lord Teika]); *Kogo Shimpishō* (Top-Secret Notes on the Words of Old); *Kyōgoku Kōmon Teikinshō* (Notes on Poetic Instruction by the Kyōgoku Middle Counselor); *Hibishō* (Ultra-Secret Notes); *Waka Hibi* (Ultra-Secret Poetics), etc.

Middle Commander Teika were sent back with marks of approval. A treatise on poetic composition was also presented. This is because [Teika] had been asked by His Excellency for private instruction on the Six Principles and the Poetic Styles."[4]

Teika's holograph is extant, except for one double sheet, which contained fifteen poems (61–68 and 77–83). (Fortunately, the entire manuscript had been copied at least once before the missing sheet was cut out.) This precious document, as valuable to the Japanese as a holograph by Chaucer of Middle English poems would be to us, is now in the collection of Mr. Ōta Fumihiro. The authenticity of the handwriting has been established beyond any doubt. This is the only extant holograph of any of Teika's treatises; it is exceptionally valuable because it establishes the *Kindai Shūka* as the only unquestionably genuine critical writing by Teika. Its existence is especially important because clever and industrious forgers began their work less than fifty years after Teika's death.[5]

The holograph has four colophons, of which only the first two are of interest. The first bears the signature and cipher of Reizei Tamehide and states, "This manuscript is in the handwriting of my great-grandfather, the Lay Priest Middle Counselor Lord Teika. It must be treasured with the utmost secrecy, the utmost secrecy." The second, added by Tamehide's pupil Imagawa Ryōshun and followed by his signature and cipher, states: "This book is in the genuine handwriting of Lord Teika. A few of the poems appear to have been left out. Perhaps this is an early draft, or perhaps it was put aside after more poems were

[4] *Azuma Kagami* in Kuroita Katsumi, ed., *Kokushi Taikei*, rev. ed., XXXII (Yoshikawa Kōbunkan, 1932), 646.

[5] Fujioka Sakutarō, in his influential history of medieval Japanese literature, *Kamakura-Muromachi Jidai Bungakushi* (Ōkura Shoten, 1915), p. 68, doubted the authenticity of all the poetic treatises attributed to Teika except the *Eiga Taigai*. Recent scholars have been accepting more and more of them as genuine. (See Ishida Yoshisada, *Fujiwara Teika no Kenkyū* [Bungadō Shoten, 1957], pp. 367–490 [hereafter Ishida].) For details of the family split after Tameie's death and the forgeries and polemic that resulted, see *JCP*, pp. 348–56.

added. The colophon shows it to have been inherited by Lord Tamehide. It is an absolutely authoritative document."

Ryōshun's statement shows that the missing pages had been cut out of the holograph at least before 1420, the date of his death, and it also suggests that Ryōshun had seen a complete version of the text. This could have been an early draft of the *Hibishō* (the most important manuscript of the *Kindai Shūka* apart from the holograph), which was probably compiled soon after Teika's death.[6] The *Hibishō* contains twenty-five poems of the version sent away, all eighty-three poems of the holograph, and the Prefatory Essay, with the exception of the first sentence found in the holograph. It is the only manuscript version of the *Kindai Shūka* that contains all the poems of the holograph.[7] Our translation is based on a collated text of the *Hibishō* and the holograph *Kindai Shūka,* which was made by Hisamatsu Sen'ichi and Nishio Minoru in 1959.

The holograph cannot be dated as precisely as the version sent away, although all evidence indicates that it dates from Teika's mid-fifties at the earliest. The style of the calligraphy is that of Teika's later years: it closely resembles the calligraphy of the extant portion of his diary for the year 1225, and also that of the holograph of his personal collection of his own poems, the *Shūi Gusō,* believed to date from 1233. In addition, scholars generally consider the *Nishidaishū* the source of all of the poems in the holograph, and internal evidence shows that the *Nishidaishū* was probably completed in 1215.[8] We may therefore assume that the holograph was written no earlier than 1215. The latest possible date of composition is of course 1241,

[6] Ishida, p. 379. Two copies of the *Hibishō* are extant. One, owned by Professor Hisamatsu Sen'ichi, is judged from the calligraphy to date from the late Muromachi period (sixteenth century).

[7] See Hisamatsu and Nishio, pp. 12–13; *Gunsho Kaidai,* IX, 129–31; and Ishida, pp. 378–79.

[8] On the relation of the *Nishidaishū* to Teika's various treatises and the date of the *Nishidaishū* itself, see Higuchi Yoshimaro, *Teika Hachidaishō to Kenkyū,* II, 66 and 118–30.

the year of Teika's death. However, an earlier *terminus ad quem* may be arrived at by comparing the holograph with Teika's *Eiga Taigai* and discovering their probable relationship.

Of all the extant treatises attributed to Teika, the *Eiga Taigai* is closest to the holograph in both structure and content. It consists of a short introductory essay written in *kambun*, i.e., in Chinese characters and syntax, and 103 exemplary poems subtitled *Shūkatei Tairyaku* (Epitome of the Styles of Superior Poems).[9] The essay is nearly identical to the second half of the *Kindai Shūka*'s Prefatory Essay, beginning rather abruptly with the prescriptive ideal of "old diction and new treatment." The selections of poems in the two works are also strikingly similar. They have seventy-two poems in common, and further, the poems in eleven groups of each (consisting of from two to eight poems) are in identical sequences. These similarities between the two anthologies are too great to be explained simply by assuming that both works are ultimately derived from the eighteen hundred poems of the *Nishidaishū*. One must therefore conclude that Teika used one work as the basis for the other. And although it cannot be proved conclusively, recent Japanese scholarship holds that the *Eiga Taigai* was based on the *Kindai Shūka*, and that a *terminus ad quem* may be established for the *Kindai Shūka* by dating the *Eiga Taigai*.[10]

According to a tradition deriving from the poet-priest Ton'a, in the early fourteenth century, the *Eiga Taigai* was written for and sent to "the Kajii Prince," the Cloistered Imperial Prince Sonkai (1204–46), a son of Go-Toba.[11] Hosokawa Yūsai, a sixteenth-century poet-scholar of the Nijō school, wrote that the *Eiga Taigai* was sent to Sonkai when Teika was sixty years old, that is, in 1222.[12] Since Sonkai's achievements as a poet are well

[9] Japanese texts of the introductory essay to the *Eiga Taigai* existed from a very early date. See Ishida, pp. 395–99.

[10] See Ishida, pp. 376–79; Hisamatsu, *Wakashi*, III, 90.

[11] See Ton'a's *Seiashō*, in *NKGT*, V, 19.

[12] Ishida, p. 389.

known, it is reasonable to assume that he was the recipient of the *Eiga Taigai*. On several counts, Yūsai's date also seems reasonable. Sonkai would have been about eighteen years old at the time, the most appropriate age for him to seek Teika's instruction. (Sanetomo received the original version of the *Kindai Shūka* when he was about the same age.) He is not likely to have requested the treatise much before 1221 because Teika was in ill favor with Go-Toba, and both Sonkai and Teika would have hesitated to be in such formal communication until the ex-Emperor had been exiled, after the Jōkyū War of 1221. It is probably safe to assume, then, that the holograph *Kindai Shūka* was completed sometime between 1215 (when the *Nishidaishū* was completed) and 1222 (the assumed date for completion of the *Eiga Taigai*).

But the question remains: for what purpose and for whom did Teika prepare the holograph *Kindai Shūka*? Professor Ishida Yoshisada thinks it wholly unlikely that Sonkai would have been presented with the *Kindai Shūka* in addition to the *Eiga Taigai*. Nor is the *Kindai Shūka* the kind of compilation that Teika would have made simply for reference; for that purpose he would have required a larger collection, such as the *Nishidaishū*. And, Ishida feels, it is not likely that Teika would have made it for his descendants, who presumably would have had access to a draft of the Prefatory Essay and to his other critical writings and anthologies, which include most of the poems of the *Kindai Shūka*. Ishida is also disturbed by the discrepancy between the Prefatory Essay, with its emphasis upon poets of the recent past, and the exemplary poems, with their stronger emphasis upon the Early Classical Period. He finally concludes that the holograph probably represents only an early stage in the production of the *Eiga Taigai*—that it was not sent to anyone, but was put aside and more or less forgotten by Teika once he had completed the *Eiga Taigai*.[13]

13 *Ibid.*, pp. 372–79.

Instructive as Professor Ishida's views are, we cannot accept
them without qualification. First, we do not feel that the dis-
crepancy between the Prefatory Essay and the poems of the
holograph is nearly so great as it appears to him—certainly not
great enough to disconcert anyone for whom the treatise might
have been written. Teika emphasized by his selection of poems
two great ages of Japanese poetry, the Early Classical Period
and the recent past, and these are precisely the two periods that
he praises in his Prefatory Essay. In the holograph he greatly
expanded the period represented by the poems, but he did not
thereby introduce intolerable discord between the poems and
the essay written years before. Only the title, *Superior Poems of
Our Time,* is disturbingly inappropriate. Second, as we sought
to show in the Introduction, the *Kindai Shūka* has a dramatic
development and unity of tone unmatched by the *Eiga Taigai.*
The poems of the *Eiga Taigai* are arranged with less attention
to overall effect and thematic harmony. This difference clearly
suggests that the *Eiga Taigai* is not a refined or expanded ver-
sion of the *Kindai Shūka,* but a separate work (notwithstanding
the fact that Teika probably used his holograph as a major
source in compiling it). The colophons of both Ryōshun and
Tamehide also indicate that the holograph was considered an
important independent work. Ryōshun's colophon was prob-
ably an attempt to account for the missing pages by suggesting
that the manuscript may have been a draft, and not the basis
for a different work. The colophons also suggest that the holo-
graph may have been among the precious manuscripts that
Abutsu the Nun jealously guarded from the senior Nijō line
of Teika's descendants and passed on to the junior Reizei line,
the descendants of her eldest son by Tameie, Reizei Tamesuke.
Such a history would help explain the relative paucity of manu-
script copies of the holograph, for permission to make copies
would have been rarely granted.

In our present state of knowledge we can only guess who may

139

have been the intended recipient of the holograph *Kindai Shū-ka*. However, we cannot help feeling that Professor Ishida dismisses rather too quickly the possibility that Teika compiled it for his immediate family, perhaps for Tameie. If it was written between 1215 and 1222, Tameie would have been between seventeen and twenty-four years old—just the age to profit from it. The young Tameie was expected eventually to inherit Teika's position as the master of Japan's supreme poetic house, but he was not particularly gifted or interested in poetry, and his training was no better than that of Teika's other pupils. It is at least possible that Teika wrote the holograph expressly to encourage Tameie in his much delayed poetic training. Tradition holds that Tameie, for his part, was depressed at the prospect of having to succeed to the position laid out for him by his father. At the age of twenty-four he decided to become a priest instead, but he was dissuaded by the Abbot Jien, himself a famous poet, who told Tameie he was still too young for it to be at all certain that he would be a failure, and urged him to devote himself to the serious study and practice of poetry. Tameie agreed and, in five days, composed a sequence of 1,000 poems. Teika expressed his satisfaction, and thus Tameie's future was decided.[14] Perhaps it is more than coincidence, more than the fact that it expresses a traditional view of poetry, that Tameie's own treatise, the *Yakumo Kuden* or *Eiga Ittei*, opens with the statement, "I have been taught that the composition of poetry does not necessarily depend upon breadth of learning, but arises solely from the heart."[15]

[14] Ton'a, *Seiashō*, in *NKGT*, V, 99.
[15] Fujiwara Tameie, *Yakumo Kuden*, in *NKGT*, III, 388.

GLOSSARY OF LITERARY TERMS

For more detailed discussion of these terms, see Japanese Court Poetry, pp. 11–15 and 503–14.

ALLUSIVE VARIATION. *Honkadori.* The echoing of the words, situation, or conception of a well-known poem in a way that evokes the earlier poem but incorporates recognizable elements of it into a new meaning. The response to the original poem's situation, tone, and meaning distinguishes this technique from simple borrowing. See, for example, poem 38, above.

HEADNOTE. *Kotobagaki.* A note, sometimes in Chinese, that precedes the poem and describes in detail the circumstances (sometimes fictional) in which the poem was composed. Some headnotes merely give the topic (*dai*), state that the topic is unknown, or hint at allegorical meanings. Other headnotes, however, are very extended and provide a prose context for the poems they introduce.

PILLOW-WORD. *Makurakotoba.* A conventional epithet or attribute for a word, usually occupying a five-syllable line and modifying the first word of the next line. The meaning of some pillow-words is uncertain. They lend a formal dignity to the style of a poem and, when their meaning is known, serve almost like images to enrich the tone. For example, *hisakata no* (distant?) is a conventional epithet for *sora* (sky), *hikari* (light), etc.

PIVOT-WORD. *Kakekotoba.* A word used within overlapping rhetorical and syntactical schemes in such a way that it takes on two or more simultaneous meanings. See, for example, poem 6, in which *nagame* is used to mean both "reverie" and "long rain."

PREFACE. *Jo, Jokotoba, Joshi.* A section of unspecified length that precedes the main statement in the poem and is joined to it by

141

wordplay, similarity of sound, or an implied metaphorical relationship. See, for example, poem 3.

TANKA. Short poem. A poetic form of 31 syllables in five lines: 5, 7, 5, 7, 7. Also known as *uta* or *waka*; waka, however, may also signify all forms of Court poetry, as distinct from its later derivatives (*renga* and *haiku*), and from popular songs and religious hymns.

WORD ASSOCIATION. *Engo.* The relation of disparate elements in a poem by the use of a word that has or creates "association" with a preceding word, often by wordplay. For example, in poem 50, *uru* means "obtain," but a homophone meaning "sell" is also suggested by association with *ichi* (market), which precedes it in the poem.

BIBLIOGRAPHY

The Bibliography is in two parts. The first lists the major sources consulted in preparing this book, apart from standard reference works. The second contains citations and brief descriptions of anthologies by Teika, listed in approximate chronological order, in which poems of the Kindai Shūka also appear. Unless otherwise specified, the place of publication is Tokyo.

Sources

Brower, Robert H., and Earl Miner. *Japanese Court Poetry*. Stanford, Calif.: Stanford University Press, 1961.

Gotō Shigeo. "*Shinkokinwakashū* koinobu no hairetsu ni kansuru ichikōsatsu," *Nagoya Daigaku Bungakubu Kenkyū Ronshū*, XXV (1961), 29–58.

Higuchi Yoshimaro, ed. "*Hachidaishū Shūitsu kō*," *Aichi Gakugei Daigaku Kenkyū Hōkoku (Jimbun Kagaku)*, No. 4 (December 1954), pp. 12–20. The only modern edition of Teika's *Hachidaishū Shūitsu*.

——, ed. *Teika Hachidaishō to Kenkyū*. 2 vols. Toyohashi: Mikan Kokubun Shiryō Kankōkai, 1956–57. In *Mikan Kokubun Shiryō*, Series 1. A collated text, with an introduction, of Teika's *Nishidaishū*.

Hisamatsu Sen'ichi. *Chūsei Wakashi (Wakashi*, Vol. III). *Tōkyōdō*, 1961. The third volume, dealing with the medieval period, of a projected five-volume history of waka.

—— and Nishio Minoru, eds. *Karonshū Nōgakuronshū*. Iwanami Shoten, 1961. Vol. LXV in *NKTBT*. This provides the most authoritative texts for Teika's *Kindai Shūka* and *Eiga Taigai*, which are accompanied by brief introductions and numerous notes. It also

Bibliography

contains, among other works, Teika's *Maigetsushō*, Go-Toba's *Go-Toba no In Gokuden*, and Kamo no Chōmei's *Mumyōshō*. Cited as Hisamatsu and Nishio.

———, Yamazaki Toshio, and Gotō Shigeo, eds. *Shinkokinwakashū.* Iwanami Shoten, 1958. In *NKTBT*.

Ishida Yoshisada. *Fujiwara Teika no Kenkyū.* Bungadō Shoten, 1957. The most detailed modern account of Teika and his works.

———, ed. *Shinkokinwakashū Zenchūkai.* Yūseidō, 1960. This edition has more detailed notes than the 1958 edition by Hisamatsu et al.

Kazamaki Keijirō. *Nihon Bungakushi no Kenkyū.* 2 vols. Kadokawa Shoten, 1961. A collection of previously published essays on Japanese literature, including two articles on the *Kindai Shūka*.

———. *Shinkokin Jidai.* Hanawa Shobō, 1955. A collection of previously published essays on the poets and poetry of the age of the *Shinkokinshū*, including an important article on the *Kindai Shūka*.

Kojima Yoshio. *Shinkokinwakashū no Kenkyū.* 2 vols. Hoshino Shoten, 1944, 1946.

Kokusho Kankōkai. *Meigetsuki.* 3 vols. 1911–12. The only modern printed edition of Teika's diary.

Konishi Jin'ichi. "Association and Progression: Principles of Integration in Anthologies and Sequences of Japanese Court Poetry, A.D. 900–1350," *Harvard Journal of Asiatic Studies*, XXI (1958), 67–127.

Kubota Utsubo, ed. *Kambon Shinkokinwakashū Hyōshaku.* 3 vols. Tōkyōdō, 1964. A complete text with detailed notes; it supersedes the editor's authoritative but incomplete *Shinkokinwakashū Hyōshaku* (2 vols., Tōkyōdō, 1932–33).

———, ed. *Kokinwakashū Hyōshaku.* Rev. ed. 3 vols. Tōkyōdō, 1960. Detailed notes.

Matsushita Daizaburō and Watanabe Fumio, compilers. *Kokka Taikan.* 2 vols. Kyōbunsha, 1903 and often reprinted. The standard index to the poems of the *Man'yōshū*, the twenty-one imperial anthologies, and other collections and sources of Court poetry.

Murayama Shūichi. *Fujiwara Teika.* Rev. ed. Yoshikawa Kōbunkan, 1962. In *Jimbutsu Sōsho*. The best short biography of Teika.

Nihon Koten Bungaku Taikei. 98 vols. to date; Iwanami Shoten, 1957–67. The most important contemporary series of annotated texts of pre-modern Japanese literature; it contains several items listed separately in this Bibliography. Cited as *NKTBT*.

Saeki Umetomo, ed. *Kokinwakashū.* Iwanami Shoten, 1958. Included in *NKTBT*.

Sasaki Nobutsuna, ed. *Nihon Kagaku Taikei.* Rev. ed., with supple-

Bibliography

ment by Kyūsōjin Hitaku. 13 vols. to date; Kazama Shobō, 1957–67. The most important collection of pre-modern works relating to Japanese poetic criticism. Vol. III includes both versions of the *Kindai Shūka*, along with most of Teika's other short anthologies and critical writings; the Introductions to each volume contain valuable information about each work. Cited as *NKGT*.

Takagi Ichinosuke, Gomi Tomohide, and Ōno Susumu, eds. *Man'yōshū*. 4 vols. Iwanami Shoten, 1957–62. In *NKTBT*. A recent scholarly edition, with valuable notes.

Yamagishi Tokuhei, ed. *Hachidaishū Zenchū*. 3 vols. Yūseidō, 1960. An edition of Kitamura Kigin's seventeenth-century *Hachidaishū Shō*, with added biographical and other indexes. Although the scholarship is three centuries old, the work is indispensable for the second through the seventh imperial anthologies, of which there are no complete, modern, annotated editions.

Teika's Anthologies

Teika Jittei. A collection of 286 poems, mostly from the *Shinkokinshū*, grouped under the ten styles Teika distinguishes in his *Maigetsushō*. It was long considered a forgery, but recent scholars have put forth convincing arguments for its authenticity. It is now believed to have been compiled between about 1207 and 1213. It is published in *NKGT*, IV, 362–79.

Nishidaishū. Teika's large selection of poems from the first eight imperial anthologies. The current title was given to the collection in later times; Teika seems to have intended calling it *Hachidaishō* or *Hachidaishū Shō*. There are some minor differences between the two main families of texts, which are believed to stem from a semifinal and a final draft. The only modern printed edition is the one edited by Higuchi Yoshimaro; it contains 1,811 poems in twenty books.

Eiga Taigai. See the Appendix, pp. 137–40. Printed texts are in Hisamatsu and Nishio, pp. 114–23, and in *NKGT*, III, 339–45. A partial translation into English of the *Eiga Taigai's* introductory essay may be found in Wm. Theodore de Bary et al., eds., *Sources of Japanese Tradition* (New York: Columbia University Press, 1958), pp. 183–84.

Shūka no Daitai. An anthology of 112 poems from the *Kokinshū*, *Gosenshū*, *Shūishū*, and *Shinkokinshū* believed to have been selected by Teika for ex-Emperor Go-Horikawa, probably after 1226. It is printed in *NKGT*, III, 355–61.

Bibliography

Hyakunin Shūka. An anthology probably compiled between 1229 and 1236 at the request of Utsunomiya Yoritsuna. The poems were originally written on separate sheets of fine paper to be pasted on the doors of Yoritsuna's villa. Since, despite its title, the collection contains 101 poems by 101 poets, including Teika, it is likely that Teika at first modestly omitted any of his own poems and was later prevailed upon by Yoritsuna to include one. The collection has ninety-seven poems in common with the *Hyakunin Isshu.* It is printed in *NKGT,* III, 362–67.

Hachidaishū Shūitsu. An anthology of eighty poems, probably compiled in 1234. The poems are Teika's selection of ten of the best poems from each of the first eight imperial anthologies. The only modern text is that edited by Higuchi Yoshimaro.

Hyakunin Isshu. (Also known as *Ogura Hyakunin Isshu*). This is the best-known short anthology of Japanese Court poetry. It was memorized by nearly every literate person from the early seventeenth century to recent times, thanks to a popular New Year's card game based on it. Many modern scholars have doubted its authenticity, but recently it has become more widely accepted as genuine. In current editions it contains one hundred poems in rough chronological order. These poems, like the *Hyakunin Shūka,* may have been intended to adorn a set of doors—perhaps at Teika's own villa—and it is possible that this work was a revision of the earlier one. It was probably completed in 1237 and then revised by Teika and by his descendants. It is available in numerous editions and may also be found in *NKGT,* III, 368–73. There are also several complete and partial translations of it into English and other Western languages; the best one is Clay McCauley's complete translation in *Hyakunin-isshu and Nori no hatsu-ne* (Yokohama: Kelly and Walsh, 1917).

INDEX OF FIRST LINES

Akeba mata, 86
Akikaze ni, 64
Aki no ta no, 62
Aki no tsuki, 60
Aki no tsuyu ya, 58
Akishino ya, 70
Ama no hara, 72
Amatsukaze, 124
Ariake no, 106
Asaborake, 74
Asajifu no, 90
Ashihiki no, 110
Au koto wa, 110
Aware ika ni, 56
Azumaji no, 90

Chigiriki na, 114
Chigiri okishi, 124

Furusato wa, 72

Hajime yori, 13
Hana no iro wa, 52
Haru tatsu to, 26, 48
Hisakata no, 54
Honobono to, 68

Ika ni sen, 92
Ima kon to, 108
Iso no kami, 74
Iza kyō wa, 50

Kagiri areba, 80
Karakoromo, 98
Kataito o, 102
Kimi ga yo wa, 76
Kimi kozu wa, 70

Kimi o okite, 114n
Koi seji to, 114
Kono yo nite, 82
Kore ya kono, 128
Kuma mo naki, 120

Mi-Kumano no, 116
Minahito wa, 78
Miwa no yama, 116
Morasu na yo, 88
Morotomo ni, 78

Nagaraeba, 126
Nageke tote, 120
Naki hito no, 80
Naki na nomi, 96
Nakiwataru, 60
Naniwabito, 84
Naniwae no, 88
Naniwagata, 94
Nao tanome, 124n
Natorigawa, 108
Natsu no yo wa, 54

Okitsukaze, 122
Okuyama ni, 66
Omoigawa, 96
Omoigusa, 104
Omoiide yo, 118
Omoiki ya, 104
Oto ni kiku, 100

Saga no yama, 122
Sakura chiru, 45n
Sakuragari, 52
Sakura saku, 50
Samushiro ni, 106

Samushiro ya, 8
Saoshika no, 66
Sasa no ha wa, 70n
Shiratsuyu mo, 68
Shiratsuyu ni, 62
Shirotae no, 8
Sode hijite, 45n
Sode no tsuyu mo, 118
Sue no tsuyu, 76
Suminoe no, 122n
Sumiwabiba, 126
Sumiwabinu, 126n
Sumiyoshi no, 112

Tachikaeri, 86
Tachiwakare, 82
Ta ga misogi, 128
Takasago no, 100
Toshi no uchi ni, 26
Tsuki mireba, 58
Tsuki ya aranu, 45n
Tsutsumedo mo, 102

Ukarikeru, 94

Wabinureba, 112
Waga io wa, 116n
Wakuraba ni, 84

Yaemugura, 56
Yamazakura, 48
Yo no naka yo, 130
Yūgure wa, 46n
Yura no to o, 98
Yū sareba, 64
Yūzukuyo, 92

INDEX OF POETS

All poets are indexed by their given names.

Akisuke (Fujiwara), 100
Anonymous, 46n, 52, 60, 64, 72, 84n,
    90n, 92, 102, 106, 108, 114, 114n,
    116n, 124n (attributed to the Bud-
    dhist divinity Kannon), 128
Asayasu (Bunya), 62

Chisato (Ōe), 58

Egyō, Priest, 56, 72(?)

Fukayabu (Kiyowara), 54

Go-Toba, ex-Emperor, 50, 58, 80, 118

Henjō, Bishop, 76, 78, 124
Hitomaro (Kakinomoto), 70n;
    attributed to, 66, 96, 110
Hitoshi (Minamoto), 90

Ietaka (Fujiwara), 86, 118
Ise, Lady, 94, 96, 116
Izumi Shikibu, Lady, 78

Kii, Lady, 100
Kiyosuke (Fujiwara), 70, 126
Komachi (Ono), 52
Korenori (Sakanoue), 74, 102
Koretada (Fujiwara), 98

Michinobu (Fujiwara), 80
Mitsune (Ōshikōchi), 122n
Motokata (Ariwara), 26
Motonaga, Prince, 110, 112
Motosuke (Kiyowara), 114
Mototoshi (Fujiwara), 124

Narihira (Ariwara), 45n, 126n

Saigyō, Priest, 56, 70, 82, 120
Saneakira (Minamoto), 68
Sarumaru Dayū (?), 66
Shunrai (Minamoto), 48, 88, 94, 104
Shunzei (Fujiwara), 84, 86, 92, 104,
    126, 130
Sosei, Priest, 50, 108, 128

Tadamichi (Fujiwara), 60
Tadamine (Mibu), 26, 48, 106
Teika (Fujiwara), 8, 13
Tenchi, Emperor, attributed to, 62
Tomonori (Ki), 54
Toshiyuki (Fujiwara), 112
Tsunenobu (Minamoto), 64, 76, 122
Tsurayuki (Ki), 45n, 68

Yoshitada (Sone), 98
Yoshitsune (Fujiwara), 74, 88
Yukihira (Ariwara), 82, 84, 122